REPAIR & RENOVATE

walls&ceilings

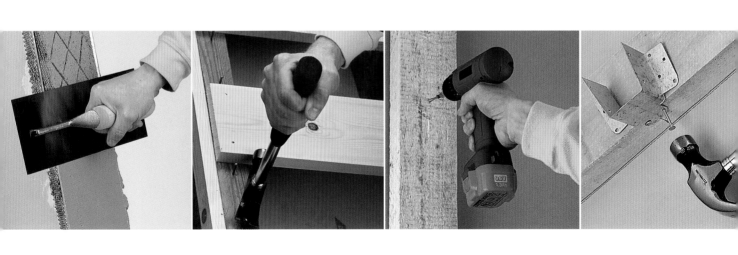

REPAIR & RENOVATE

walls&ceilings

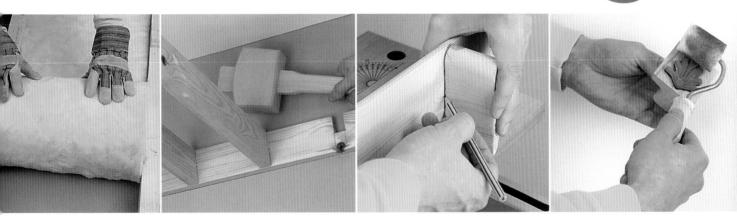

Julian Cassell & Peter Parham

TIME
LIFE
BOOKS

Alexandria, Virginia

Glass-block walls make stunning room features and are remarkably easy to construct, see page 62

Decorative paneling is simple to apply and helps to protect wall surfaces, see page 100

introduction

Home improvement is fast becoming a national pastime with more and more people tackling jobs that would previously have been left to the services of professional tradesmen. Taking on a job yourself can be cheaper and more rewarding than hiring a person—ensuring that the finished effect is actually how you imagined and falls within a budget that does not incur additional labor costs.

repair & renovation issues

This revolution has been fuelled by a booming DIY retail sector, which tries to convince us that no job is too difficult and any practically-minded person can set about full-scale home renovation. Although it is true to say that there is huge scope for applying oneself to home improvement tasks, it is always important to know your limitations right from the outset. It is best to approach DIY as a learning curve, building up your experience and knowledge before tackling jobs of greater difficulty. This book concerns itself with renovation and repairs in your home that are directly related to two of the major structural elements in all houses—the walls and the ceilings.

Repair issues can be neatly separated from those of renovation—the former is concerned primarily with making good existing features, and the latter is related to adjusting the appearance of certain areas in your home. Renovation therefore clearly leans more heavily on the creative side of your abilities, whereas repairs generally tend to be dependent on your ability to apply yourself practically to restoring a particular finish or structure.

Most people are able to recognize when a particular area of their home needs adapting or changing, but realizing or imagining what that change should be exactly can often be a more difficult process. Therefore, inspiration for change needs to be balanced with the potential options available, which in turn relate firmly to budget, personal choice, your ability to tackle the work, and how much professional advice or input may be required for the task. It is best to try and tackle each of these areas in turn.

The smallest of renovation or home improvement tasks will always cost some money and therefore it is impossible to begin work without deciding on a budget. This prime area for concern is covered in more detail in Chapter 2, but right from the initial stages, budgetary constraints will be the major governing factor in deciding on the extent of work.

Personal choice is clearly of the utmost importance when you come to repairing and renovating your house. Work out your ideal situation, and then compromise according to the wishes of other people who will be affected and the relative value of your house. Although most of the variable sales points in a house relate to fixtures such as bathroom and kitchen fittings, decisions on wall or ceiling structure will certainly affect the look of your house and therefore the appearance to a potential buyer. So decide whether your plans are to renovate purely to cater to your needs, or whether you

LEFT *Building a pass-through between two rooms adds an attractive and practical design feature, while also allowing more light into what may otherwise be a dark area of your home.*

RIGHT *Where structural considerations allow, a glass-block wall offers a striking and stylish alternative to more traditional wall design, allowing a wash of light into a room.*

are aiming to provide a general level of improvement that will also appeal to others.

Next comes the question of your ability to tackle home improvement tasks. This book takes into account a wide variety of options and techniques covering all aspects of ceiling and wall renovation. However, some techniques are clearly more demanding than others, and therefore it is important to evaluate your capabilities. It is always advisable to have a source for some professional advice when needs dictate, even if it is just to provide a guiding hand rather than full-scale employment. The areas of plumbing and electric are specific examples where professional help will almost certainly be required, especially when such services need rerouting or customizing to adapt to your new room layout. There is also a clear safety issue here as it is never advisable to tackle any such work unless you have the relevant qualifications and experience in these areas. Safety is therefore one area where there is no room for compromise when renovating your home.

difficulty rating

The following symbols are designed to give an indication of difficulty level relating to particular tasks and projects in this book. Clearly what are simple jobs to one person may be difficult to another and vice versa. These guidelines are primarily based on the ability of an individual in relation to the experience required and degree of technical ability.

Straightforward and requiring limited technical skills

Straightforward but requiring a reasonable skill level

Technically quite difficult, and could involve a number of skills

High skill level required, and involves a number of techniques

wall & ceiling consideration

By their very nature, walls and ceilings are the largest surface areas in your home, and so they can be the defining factor in general appearance. Much of this finished look will be due to the finishes applied, but the actual layout and design of your home will supply the framework for these finishes and therefore the effect that is produced. In addition to personal tastes, sympathetic consideration should be given towards the basic architecture, period and style of your home. For example, however much fun the idea of installing suspended ceilings in a period house may sound to you, it may not hold such an irresistible desire for someone else—thus you not only lose the natural features in your home, you may also inhibit your chance to sell at a later date. So there is a fine line to be observed between taste and personal flare, and it is always best to take time when considering your ideas before seeking to implement them.

Most people have considered changing walls or their features in some way, but ceilings have always tended to be a neglected area when it comes to home improvement. They are often dismissed at the planning stage, and are simply considered as an area that will literally "get a coat of paint" once the actual construction of the project is complete. Therefore this book does tend to emphasize that not all home improvement options relate to wall position and coverings, and there are a multitude of options for ceiling renovation, which relate both to the efficiency of its structure and the decorative or design aspects that it can portray. Ceilings must therefore be considered as an integral part of the look of your home and shouldn't be sidelined as an area that will simply follow a trend—rather, see them as a surface that can add to and complement the general room and home design.

Safety issues are obviously a vital issue, particularly as the structural makeup of homes can vary so widely because of age and style. It is important to understand the structure of your home fully before embarking on renovation work, and issues of ceiling and wall structure are covered in considerable detail in the early chapters of this book.

Repair and renovation projects may therefore be as large or small in scale as you wish, and anybody can tackle

different DIY tasks around the home according to their own capabilities. This book helps to break down many of the myths or complications surrounding ceiling and wall renovation and repair, and aims to provide clear guidelines on producing looks and finishes that you may not have realized you were capable of achieving. For the best results, try to follow the order of this book as it takes you through a correct order of work, right from the "Anatomy of Walls and Ceilings" in chapter 1, through the planning stages of chapter 2 and onto projects that follow. Each of the projects relates specifically to the different areas and options regarding your walls and ceilings.

Above all, you should enjoy working on renovation and repair projects in your home for if they are completed successfully, you will be enhancing the appearance and living space of your home, while also adding to its value.

RIGHT *Strong colors will always emphasize the texture and design of wall and ceiling structures.*

BELOW LEFT *Paneling has enjoyed a revival in popularity and may be used on both walls and ceilings.*

Using this book

The layout of this book has been designed to provide project instruction in as comprehensive yet straightforward a manner as possible. The illustration below provides a general guideline to the different elements incorporated into this design. Full-color photos and diagrams combined with explanatory text, laid out in a clear, step-by-step order, provide easy-to-follow instructions. Boxes drawing your attention to safety issues, general tips, and alternative options accompany each project.

color-coordinated tabs help you quickly find your place again when moving between chapters

at the beginning of each job a list of tools is provided

options boxes offer extra instruction on techniques related to the project in hand

diagrams help to explain structural or design issues

safety boxes, pink for emphasis, draw attention to safety considerations

tip boxes have been used to provide helpful hints, developed from professional experience, on how to achieve particular tasks

anatomy of walls & ceilings

Many factors affect the anatomy or makeup of the walls and ceilings in your home. Some differences relate to age, with issues that were once common building practice or regulation now being out of date or superseded by improved design and modern materials. Architectural preference can also make a significant difference, which means that even buildings of the same age can have entirely different wall or ceiling structures. So, before embarking on a renovation project, it is important to try and recognize the different types of house structure, so that you can make informed decisions on the extent and type of work that will be required. This chapter considers the most common varieties of wall and ceiling anatomy and how they are constructed.

Open-plan living can be extended to split-level designs, where the "open" theme continues over more than one floor level.

11

house construction

Ceilings and walls are, quite obviously, major components of a house's structure. So before embarking on any alterations, it's important to examine the makeup of your house in its entirety. This will help you to recognize some of the main design features and form a greater understanding of the structure of your home and its particular characteristics.

Most modern houses are referred to either as brick and block or wood-framed. However, there are wide variations on this theme, and older buildings may include a number of different structures and features. Understanding the principles of house construction can help with recognizing some of your home's characteristics.

It's important to remember that, regardless of house design, the role of walls can be isolated to one key feature —whether they are load-bearing or non-load-bearing. Non-load-bearing walls act as a partition and do not bear any of the house weight, whereas load-bearing walls play an integral part in supporting the structure and bearing the weight of floors. This theme is common to all houses and is the starting point for deciding on any alterations.

tips of the trade

It can sometimes be difficult to identify a wall that is load-bearing.

• Assume that all exterior walls are load-bearing.

• Check where floorboards run parallel with a wall. This implies that the joists run in the opposite direction (ie, at right angles), and are supported by the wall.

• Look in the attic to see if roof members sit on top of the wall. If so, support for the roof is being supplied by that wall.

• Cut a small hole in the ceiling at the top of the wall to allow you to inspect the wall construction, to see where joists are running, and to see how much support the wall is creating.

• Look for joist termination directly on top of the wall.

understanding wood & block

The majority of houses combine wood, blocks, or bricks in their construction and any of these components can have a load-bearing role to play. In other words, a wall that is wood-framed is as capable of being load-bearing as a wall that is made from block or bricks. Similarly, a wall made of brick or blocks does not, necessarily, have to be load-bearing.

The common misconception that a wood-frame wall has less of a load-bearing capability than one made from solid block or brick must therefore be totally dispelled. Instead of judging walls by the material they are made of, it is more useful to think of walls in terms of the role they play within the total house structure (see the illustration on page 13).

brick and block houses

Modern brick houses are based on a cavity wall construction, with an outer layer of brick or block and a secondary, inner layer of brick or block. The space between the two walls is usually around 2in (50mm) wide. These houses should not be confused with older brick and block properties where the characteristics are more likely to be those specified under "solid wall construction" (right).

To ensure structural strength, the cavity between the outer and inner brick walls is spanned by special ties. If the interior wall is load-bearing, it will

be made from block or brick. If it is non-load-bearing, the internal wall may again be built with blocks, or less heavyweight stud partitioning (wood frames) may be used.

wood-framed houses

As the name suggests, the main structural elements of these houses are built using wood frames, though they are also built on a cavity structure comprised of two walls. The interior, wooden wall framework is erected first and the outer wall is then built from brick, block, or wood cladding. As with brick and block houses, the exterior walls are generally load-bearing. However, because the interior walls are made of wood, it can sometimes be difficult to determine whether these walls are load-bearing or not.

solid wall construction

This type of construction is found in older houses, where there is no cavity and therefore not a two-layer system. Walls in these houses tend to be thicker, often with the stone or brick makeup extending from the outer to the inner face of the wall. Interior walls are either made of materials similar to the exterior walls or they may be constructed from wood frame partitioning, demonstrating lath and plaster characteristics (see page 19). Load-bearing walls in these houses are nearly always the same stone or brick structure as the exterior walls.

supports

Entrances in load-bearing walls, such as windows and doors, reduce the strength of the wall. For this reason, extra support will be needed over the window or door, to bear the structural weight of the wall above. (Non-load-bearing walls do not always need this extra support.) These extra supports are either referred to as lintels, which are made of concrete or steel, or headers, which are made of wood. The type of material depends upon the age of the house, the wall construction, and the size of the opening. Modern techniques favor engineered wood framing members (such as LVL) or steel-reinforced headers in wood-framed walls, whereas reinforced concrete lintels are generally used on brick or block walls. Exterior cavity walls may combine lintel types with concrete on the outer wall and wood on the interior.

house structure

In order to understand the role and function of ceilings and walls, it can be useful to put them in the context of an entire structure. The cross section of a house shown below demonstrates the integration of walls and ceilings, and highlights those areas of the house that bear weight or help to support the weight of the building.

A non-load-bearing wall acts as a partition between rooms and has no role in weight support in the house as a whole. *See page 18*

Ceilings (roof level) are generally constructed from wooden joists. Plasterboard or drywall is affixed to the joists, providing the ceiling for the room below. *See page 15*

Opening up two rooms to make one will require a lintel or header if a load-bearing wall is being removed. *See page 42*

Non-load-bearing walls may themselves need extra support to take their weight when they run in the same direction as the floor joists. Adding an extra joist in this area is therefore vital

Doorways or entrances in non-load-bearing walls do not necessarily require a lintel because the wall does not have a weight-supporting role. *See page 48*

Floor levels between rooms may require aligning if a wall has been removed. *See page 46*

All windows will have a lintel or header of some nature to support the wall above

A load-bearing wall, as its name suggests, is an integral part of the structure of a house, supplying general support as well as carrying the weight of floors. *See page 18*

The exterior walls of most modern houses are of a cavity construction in that they comprise an outer and inner wall. These are linked together with wall ties that span the cavity. *See page 16*

Floors and ceilings between levels are generally constructed from wooden joists whose weight is supported by the exterior walls and interior load-bearing walls. *See page 14*

Doors and entrances of interior load-bearing walls will always have a header above them to provide support for the wall above

Underfloor construction varies according to foundations. The floor surface will normally consist of concrete or wood joists with some type of wood subfloor

ceiling & floor construction

The structure of a house dictates that the ceiling of a room will quite often combine to make up the floor of the room above. Since alterations to one room can thereby affect the structure of another, it is vital to consider both ceiling and floor anatomy when planning changes. All the structures shown here have wooden joists that make up the framework of the ceiling. Quite a few modern homes, however, incorporate solid concrete ceilings—so there will be some variation on the themes outlined below. As with most designs, trends vary with time and the basic ceiling structure will be very dependent on the age of the building.

lath-and-plaster ceilings

An old design, lath-and-plaster ceilings are now avoided in modern techniques of construction. However, they are still commonly found in older houses and may well feature in a house that is intended for renovation.

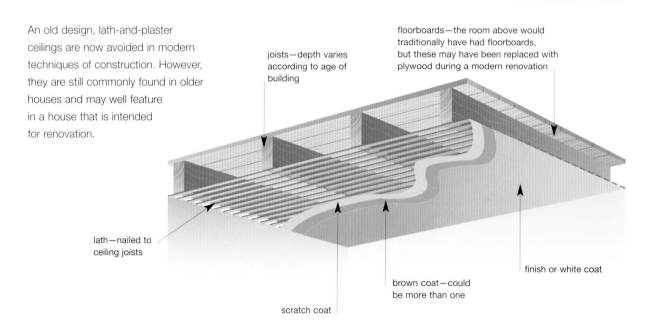

joists—depth varies according to age of building

floorboards—the room above would traditionally have had floorboards, but these may have been replaced with plywood during a modern renovation

lath—nailed to ceiling joists

finish or white coat

brown coat—could be more than one

scratch coat

plasterboard and plaster ceilings

The invention of plasterboard made lath construction an out-of-date and time-consuming method for building ceilings. Therefore, most modern ceilings have a plasterboard base, which is plastered as shown here, or a drywall base as shown on page 15.

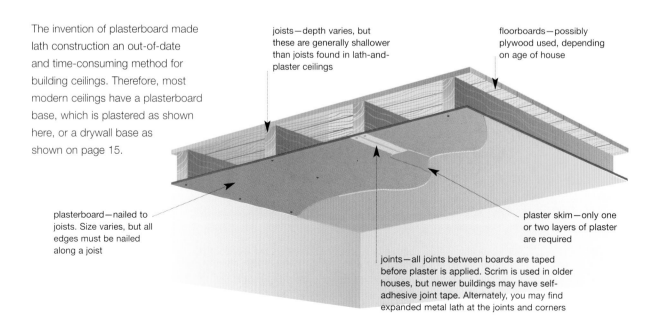

joists—depth varies, but these are generally shallower than joists found in lath-and-plaster ceilings

floorboards—possibly plywood used, depending on age of house

plasterboard—nailed to joists. Size varies, but all edges must be nailed along a joist

plaster skim—only one or two layers of plaster are required

joints—all joints between boards are taped before plaster is applied. Scrim is used in older houses, but newer buildings may have self-adhesive joint tape. Alternately, you may find expanded metal lath at the joints and corners

drywall ceilings

Although similar to plastered ceilings, drywall ceilings are finished using a slightly different technique. Drywall tape over the tapered edges seals the joint and produces a smooth surface ready to paint. This is probably the easiest ceiling structure for a home-improvement enthusiast to tackle.

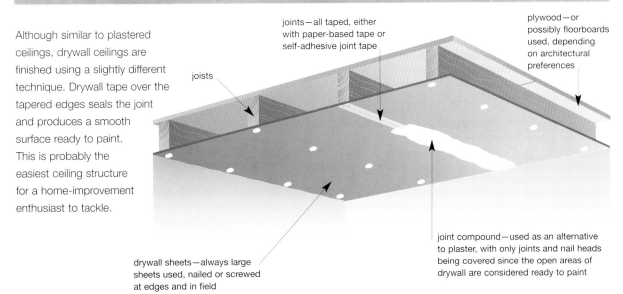

joints—all taped, either with paper-based tape or self-adhesive joint tape

plywood—or possibly floorboards used, depending on architectural preferences

joists

drywall sheets—always large sheets used, nailed or screwed at edges and in field

joint compound—used as an alternative to plaster, with only joints and nail heads being covered since the open areas of drywall are considered ready to paint

wooden ceilings

Not all ceilings have a drywall or plaster-based finish. Wood is a common alternative. Be aware, though, that wood ceilings may constitute a fire hazard unless they are installed over a drywall ceiling because air can mitigate between the room and the joist bays.

floorboards—wooden board choice for ceiling will often mean a wooden board above

joists

tongue-and-groove boards—boards interlocked to create a neat finish. The boards are nailed to joists either "invisibly" through tongues or through the board face

board lengths—join lengthwise with straight cuts measured to meet at joists

top floor ceilings

The ceiling between the top floor of a house and the attic space is often slightly different in makeup from the other ceilings in the house. The overall structure will depend on the age of the building and may therefore look like any of those already shown. The main difference will be the presence of an insulating layer between the ceiling and attic, and a basic plywood floor may be fitted on the upper layer.

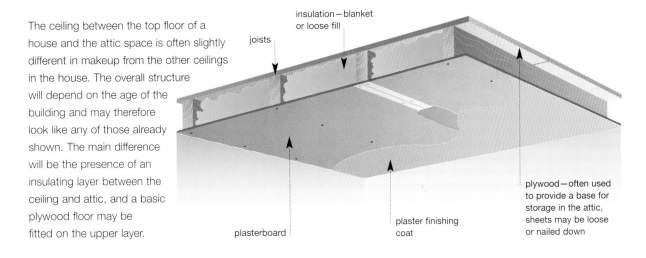

insulation—blanket or loose fill

joists

plasterboard

plaster finishing coat

plywood—often used to provide a base for storage in the attic, sheets may be loose or nailed down

exterior walls

Wall purpose and structure can be categorized as to whether the wall is interior or exterior. Much like ceilings, the age of the property can affect the type of structure considerably, as can architectural or design considerations. This is particularly the case for exterior walls, which are visible as a finished product, whereas interior walls are constructed to provide a flat surface ready for paint or wallpaper. That said, exterior walls can generally be identified by two simple categories—whether they are of a solid or cavity structure.

solid walls

Solid exterior walls, or those with no cavity, tend to be found in older buildings. Depth and makeup is varied, but most have characteristics similar to the examples outlined below.

cavity walls

Nearly all modern houses have exterior walls constructed with a cavity. This means that the exterior wall effectively consists of two layers, with a space or cavity between the layers for insulation.

There are many possible combinations for how these two layers are constructed but the examples on the following page demonstrate the most common variations that occur.

brick/block solid wall

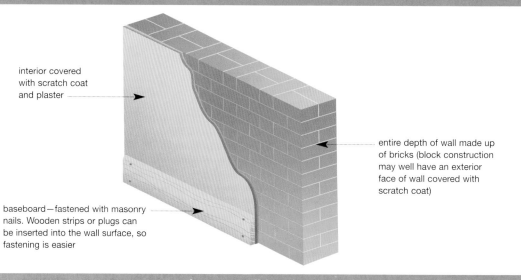

interior covered with scratch coat and plaster

entire depth of wall made up of bricks (block construction may well have an exterior face of wall covered with scratch coat)

baseboard—fastened with masonry nails. Wooden strips or plugs can be inserted into the wall surface, so fastening is easier

natural stone solid wall

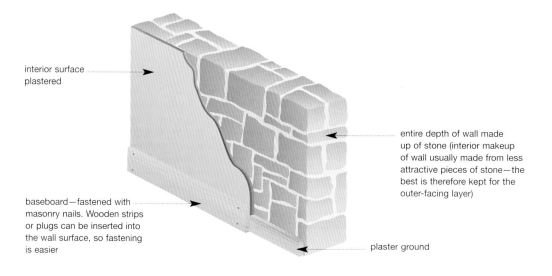

interior surface plastered

entire depth of wall made up of stone (interior makeup of wall usually made from less attractive pieces of stone—the best is therefore kept for the outer-facing layer)

baseboard—fastened with masonry nails. Wooden strips or plugs can be inserted into the wall surface, so fastening is easier

plaster ground

brick/block cavity with scratch coat & plaster

This type of cavity wall employs solid-wall construction materials to provide a brick outer layer for the finished exterior of the house and a block inner layer that requires additional coatings before paint can be applied.

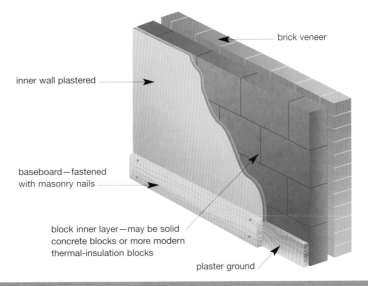

brick veneer

inner wall plastered

baseboard—fastened with masonry nails

block inner layer—may be solid concrete blocks or more modern thermal-insulation blocks

plaster ground

brick veneer

This is a popular form of construction in modern houses, where the exterior wall layer is made of a solid facing material such as brick, and the interior layer takes the form of a wooden framework.

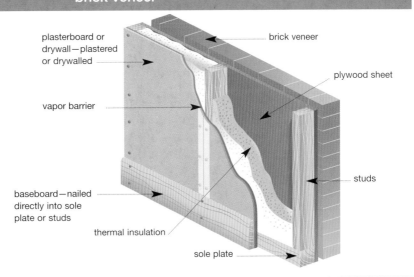

plasterboard or drywall—plastered or drywalled

brick veneer

plywood sheet

vapor barrier

baseboard—nailed directly into sole plate or studs

studs

thermal insulation

sole plate

brick/block cavity—drywalled

This example shows that block walls can be combined with drywall techniques for finishing purposes. Outer and inner wall construction is similar to that shown for the first example of cavity walls, but the internal finishing is clearly different.

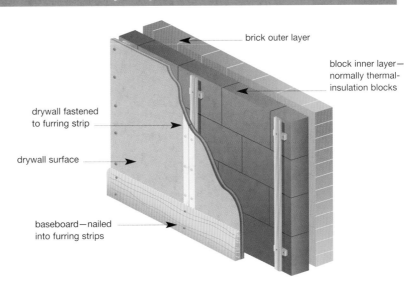

brick outer layer

block inner layer—normally thermal-insulation blocks

drywall fastened to furring strip

drywall surface

baseboard—nailed into furring strips

interior walls

Interior walls are usually constructed as a single layer and therefore do not have the same depth as exterior walls. Many characteristics are similar, but there tends to be a wide variety of structure in terms of the interior makeup of the wall itself. Much is dependent on whether the wall is load-bearing or non-load-bearing, and therefore what structural requirements it has in relation to the rest of the building.

solid construction

As the name suggests, these walls are made from solid materials, blocks or bricks. The main structural differences depend on how the outer faces of the wall are finished.

hollow construction

Hollow-wall construction is very common in modern houses, with most homes containing some form of "hollow" wall. However, this does not necessarily mean that the wall is non-load-bearing, and it is important to check out such issues before beginning the work. The examples on the page opposite illustrate the most common types of interior hollow walls.

block

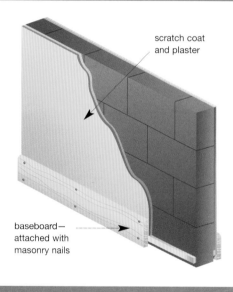

scratch coat and plaster

baseboard—attached with masonry nails

brick

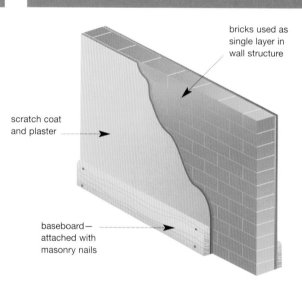

bricks used as single layer in wall structure

scratch coat and plaster

baseboard—attached with masonry nails

block/drywalled

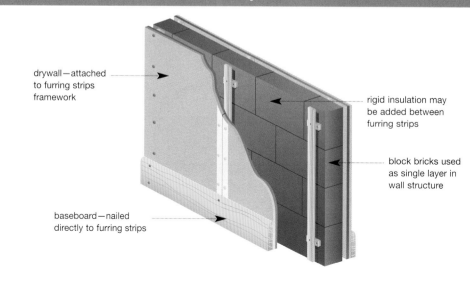

drywall—attached to furring strips framework

rigid insulation may be added between furring strips

block bricks used as single layer in wall structure

baseboard—nailed directly to furring strips

drywall/stud partition

Probably the most commonly occurring of all modern inside hollow walls. Easy to build and adaptable to most circumstances.

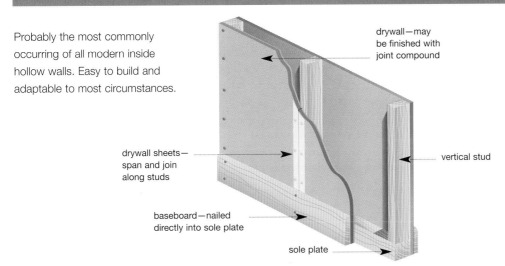

drywall—may be finished with joint compound

drywall sheets— span and join along studs

vertical stud

baseboard—nailed directly into sole plate

sole plate

dry partition wall

A lightweight and simply built wall. Its makeup still provides a rigid finished product.

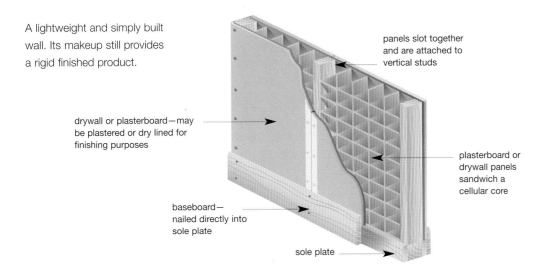

panels slot together and are attached to vertical studs

drywall or plasterboard—may be plastered or dry lined for finishing purposes

plasterboard or drywall panels sandwich a cellular core

baseboard— nailed directly into sole plate

sole plate

lath-and-plaster partition

As with ceiling structures, lath and plaster dates to houses before the advent of plasterboard or drywall.

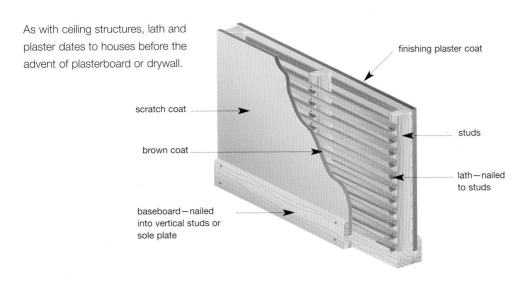

finishing plaster coat

scratch coat

brown coat

studs

lath—nailed to studs

baseboard—nailed into vertical studs or sole plate

planning

Careful planning is crucial for any type of repair or renovation because there are so many issues that need close consideration. In addition to gauging tool and material requirements, it is also important to establish whether planning permission will be necessary, whether you are capable of carrying out all the work yourself, and what the total cost and time frame will be. The extent and nature of a project will be highly dependent on at least some, if not all, of these considerations. This chapter provides some basic guidelines in all of these areas and helps to provide a framework for decision making and setting about a renovation project.

The careful use of mirrors, as shown here, can create the illusion of space for your bathroom.

options for change

The first stage of planning should focus on what currently exists in the home and what you would like to change. This can be considered as the inspirational stage, though any potential ideas must be checked against the compatibility of your existing house structure. Design inspiration can take many forms, and you may be able to picture your requirements quite easily. But, you may want to find ideas in magazines or from other people's homes.

open plan

Turning two rooms into one, or widening entrances between rooms, is a way of creating a more open layout. While providing a lighter, more spacious atmosphere, careful attention must be paid to the feasibility of removing whole or partial walls, especially if they are load-bearing. However, this sort of renovation can dramatically change the look of your home and totally transform a cramped, rather gloomy atmosphere into a design of far greater appeal. In an age where space is at a premium, every opportunity should be taken to make the best use of all areas.

RGHT *Open-plan dining and living areas create a very relaxed and comfortable feel to your home, which is appropriate to modern design and space utilization.*

bathroom options

Putting up a wall to carve a small bathroom out of bedroom space is a very popular renovation carried out in many homes. The construction considerations are straightforward, but remember to account for the expense of actually installing the bathroom and the cost of plumbing that will be incurred. Not only may you have to extend supply pipes, but you may also have new drainage requirements. The end result is invariably worth the effort, adding greater convenience and comfort to your lifestyle. This is especially the case for larger families, where the addition of an extra bathroom will ease the demand on the main bathroom.

LEFT *Although connected bathrooms may sometimes feel slightly cramped, mirrors can be used to counter this impression by creating an illusion of space.*

split-level exposure

Ceiling design need not always be restricted to a flat and two-dimensional appearance. Look at options to build split-level ceilings or, on a top floor, look at the possibility of exposing roof rafters to create a more open, airy atmosphere. Both these options require extensive work, but the results can add much greater interest to the ceiling structure as a whole.

ornate ceilings

It is not always necessary to go to great effort structurally in order to improve the appearance of a ceiling. For example, simply adding decorative effects to the existing ceiling, such as a cornice or ceiling roses, can make a dramatic improvement. These features can be installed relatively easily and provide an instant effect that "lifts" the mood of a room.

wall options

Just as ornate fittings can be added to ceilings, simple decorative features can also be applied to wall surfaces, helping to "break up" a flat, monotonous surface. Different types of wooden paneling can be used, together with various other decorative techniques such as special paint effects or natural wood systems. Manufacturers are increasingly catering to this market, producing a range of proprietary products that are inspired by traditional methods, such as paneling, and that are easy to use.

ABOVE *Open-plan living can be extended to split-level designs, where the overall "open" theme is continued over two or three levels.*

LEFT *The ornate moldings that make up this ceiling appearance add great decorative appeal to this entrance hall—an area often neglected in many households.*

BELOW *In this bathroom, the tongue-and-groove theme has been used on both the walls and ceiling, providing an unusual but well-balanced decorative scheme.*

tools & equipment

The range of tools and equipment necessary for completing DIY tasks can be vast and expensive. Yet many of the basic tools are in fact multi-purpose and make up what might be called a "household tool kit". Once this strong base of essential tools has been established, you can go on to purchase more specialized tools as and when they are required. Although it is not necessary to spend a fortune on equipment, it is generally a good rule to buy the best tools that you can afford. Top quality tools tend to last longer and give better results, time and again.

household tools

This general household tool kit contains the essential tools for carrying out any number of small jobs and tasks around the home. Although the kit will not cope with every situation you encounter, it provides a good starting point to which you can add more specific tool requirements.

claw hammer

nail set

sanding block

stud finder

wire brush

slot-head screwdrivers

Phillips head screwdrivers

insulated sleeves

utility knife

combination pliers

carpenter's pencil

side cutters

long-nose pliers

half-round rasp

general purpose chisels

oil stone

awl

cordless drill/driver

locking pliers

caulking gun

stepladder

wooden mallet

tape measure

clamp

mini hacksaw

torpedo level

scraper

miter box

hand saw

power tools

Power tools are designed to make jobs easier and less time consuming. For most enthusiasts, mid-range tools are ideal, since the very expensive equipment is designed for everyday work and the very cheap equipment for the occasional DIY person. Even so, the cost of power tools has dropped considerably, and it is possible to buy quality products relatively cheaply. For some tasks, it can even be worth buying very cheap tools for limited use before discarding.

power drill

router

jigsaw

quarter sheet sander

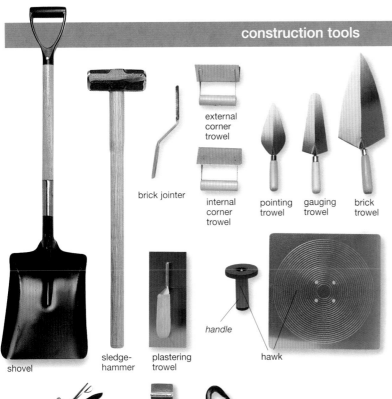

brick jointer

external corner trowel

internal corner trowel

pointing trowel

gauging trowel

brick trowel

In order to carry out alterations to walls and ceilings, the household tool kit needs to be supplemented with construction tools for heavy-duty tasks. Try to concentrate on specific needs when purchasing such tools; it can be tempting to fall for gimmicky options or cheap alternatives that will be of minimal use over the long term. Instead, stick to good quality, tried and true tools that will last for several years of DIY projects. If you are unsure of the best product, consult your retailer.

plastic bucket

shovel

sledge-hammer

plastering trowel

handle

hawk

smoothing plane

drywall saw

board and door lifter

pry bar

power stirrer or mixer

combination square

miter saw

plumb bob

chalk line

hacksaw

caulk blade

water level

spirit level

workbench

brick chisel

cold chisel

hand sledge

taping/coating knife

RENTING TOOLS

For isolated tasks that require particularly heavy-duty equipment, or tools that are very expensive to buy, renting is often the best option. This area has become a growing sector of the DIY market, and rental stores are increasingly catering to home-repair enthusiasts, as well as traditional commercial customers.

construction materials—1

The materials used in house construction are clearly wide and varied and depend on the age of the building and its design. However, there are many items that are common to most building work, with many examples shown here. The materials outlined below are the modern structural components that can be used for renovation projects—the items used to fit all these components together and "finish" them prior to painting are outlined on pages 28–9.

building boards and accessories

medium density fiberboard—better known as MDF, used as a general purpose building board. Manufactured in various thicknesses and varieties.

plasterboard—manufactured in various thicknesses and varieties. Used as a base for plaster. Drywall is a similar material.

plywood—all-purpose building board constructed from compressed wooden veneers. Manufactured in various thicknesses and varieties offering different properties.

preformed plaster or drywall arch—used as a fastened template for forming arched entrances or openings.

cove—used as decorative molding around wall/ceiling junction. More ornate forms are referred to as cornice.

brackets and bars

resilient channel— used in combination with soundproofing insulation slab on wall and ceiling surfaces.

wall profile—used as bracket to tie in new block walls with existing ones.

wall profile tie—clips to wall profile and is inserted between block courses for extra strength.
standard joist hanger
minijoist hanger

joist hangers—all these are used for supporting ends of joists at the wall junction.

corner bead—metal former used to create precise outside corners when plastering.

bricks and blocks

brick—manufactured in different colors, finishes, and general makeup, displaying varying properties and characteristics.

natural stone—used mainly in older properties but now also used in newer buildings as facing, floors or countertops

autoclaved aerated concrete block—used mainly for internal layer of cavity walls. Sometimes manufactured in greater lengths than standard block size.

glass block—decorative wall construction material. Non-load-bearing.

CMU block—used for internal layer of cavity walls and inside load-bearing or non-load-bearing walls. Sometimes manufactured with reconstructed stone facing and used for outside walls. Also sometimes used as outside wall and then plastered.

framing lumber 2 x 4in (5 x 10cm)—multi-purpose building material

dressed softwood 1 x 2in (2.5 x 5cm)—used for frameworks for trim or backer.

dressed softwood 1 x 6in (2.5 x 15cm)—common floorboard size and other multi-purpose building uses

tongue-and-groove paneling—used as paneling for wall surfaces or on ceilings. Deeper or more heavy-duty boards sometimes used for subfloor.

panel molding—decorative feature added to flush doors or to create a paneled wall effect.

chair rail—decorative rail used around perimeter of a room. Available in all sizes and many designs.

casing—decorative trim around doorways. Available in all sizes and many designs.

baseboard—decorative and protective trim at floor/wall junction. Available in all sizes and many designs.

insulation materials

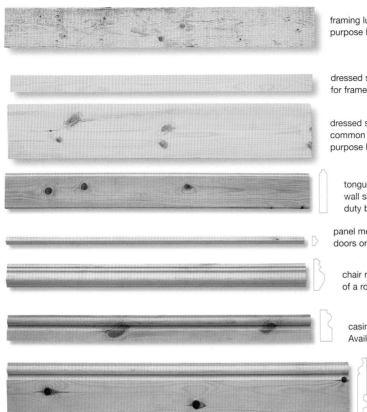

soundproofing insulation—supplied usually in 2 x 4ft (60 x 120cm) sections. Used in walls, ceilings, and floors for sound insulation.

rock wool—supplied in roll or blanket and used for thermal insulation in attic or stud walls.

loose-fill insulation—alternative to the rock wool option.

suspended ceiling system

wall angle—makes outer frame of suspended ceiling.

main tee—creates main frame of system.

ceiling tiles—fit into framework created by tee.

cross tee—fits between main bearers.

angle brackets—used to attach supporting wire to ceiling.

wire—holds framework in place, extending from main bearers to ceiling.

construction materials—2

In addition to major structural items for building projects, it is obviously necessary to have suitable materials for fastening components and for reaching a suitable finish. The materials listed here should cover the majority of tasks involved in ceiling and wall construction work, although it must be understood that there are sometimes slight variations in material design or makeup between different manufacturers, so always check with the retailer if in doubt.

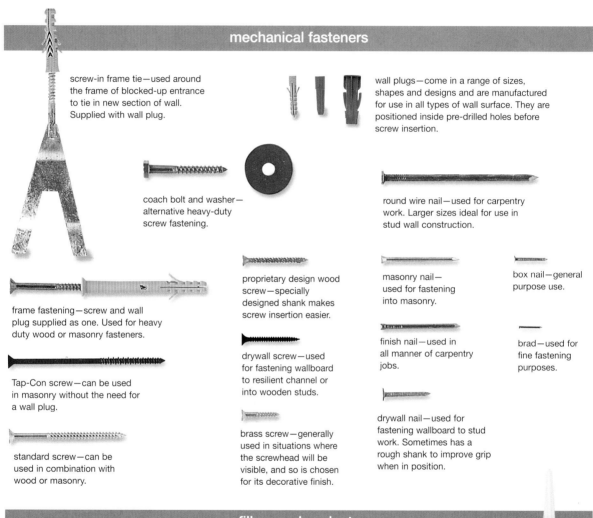

mechanical fasteners

screw-in frame tie—used around the frame of blocked-up entrance to tie in new section of wall. Supplied with wall plug.

wall plugs—come in a range of sizes, shapes and designs and are manufactured for use in all types of wall surface. They are positioned inside pre-drilled holes before screw insertion.

coach bolt and washer—alternative heavy-duty screw fastening.

round wire nail—used for carpentry work. Larger sizes ideal for use in stud wall construction.

frame fastening—screw and wall plug supplied as one. Used for heavy duty wood or masonry fasteners.

proprietary design wood screw—specially designed shank makes screw insertion easier.

masonry nail—used for fastening into masonry.

box nail—general purpose use.

Tap-Con screw—can be used in masonry without the need for a wall plug.

drywall screw—used for fastening wallboard to resilient channel or into wooden studs.

finish nail—used in all manner of carpentry jobs.

brad—used for fine fastening purposes.

standard screw—can be used in combination with wood or masonry.

brass screw—generally used in situations where the screwhead will be visible, and so is chosen for its decorative finish.

drywall nail—used for fastening wallboard to stud work. Sometimes has a rough shank to improve grip when in position.

fillers and sealants

caulk—many caulks or flexible fillers are supplied in a tubed form. Caulking gun required to expel material from tube.

all-purpose filler—multipurpose filler, mixed with water to create "paste" for filling holes in most surfaces.

joint compound—supplied ready mixed. Used for filling over taped joints and nail heads when finishing drywall.

bonding and finishing materials

bonding coat—water added and used as heavy-duty filler prior to plastering.

undercoat plaster—water added and used as undercoat to multifinish plaster.

cement—added to water with sand to create mortar for building purposes. Other general uses.

one-coat plaster—water added and used as general-purpose plaster.

textured coating—added to water to form textured coating for ceilings or walls.

building sand—added to cement and water to create mortar for building purposes. Other connected uses.

multifinish plaster—water added and used as top-coat finishing plaster.

fine sand—used for some mortar requirements and general-purpose use.

adhesives

plasticizer—added to mortar to improve ease of use.

tapes

corner joint tape—used when finishing interior or exterior corners.

joint tape—covers joints between wallboard sheets.

masking tape—used to mask surfaces before painting or to temporarily hold lightweight objects in position.

self-adhesive joint tape—used to cover joints between drywall sheets. Easy to apply.

electrical tape—multipurpose PVC tape.

sound/heat insulation tape—used around ceiling/wall junctions and/or door and window surrounds.

bonding agent—multi-purpose adhesive used in concentrated or dilute forms.

wood glue—for sticking together wooden surfaces.

29

how to start

Before commencing any project, it is important to plan your overall approach to the job and a specific order of work. Simple repairs or minor renovations tend not to raise too many problems, but inadequate planning on larger scale projects can produce very real difficulties. Even if the physical work itself is organized, issues such as building regulations and planning permission may need to be addressed.

planning permission

Before any construction project can begin, some consideration must be given to whether the particular work will need planning permission. The majority of projects inside the home do not need planning approval, and so this is not an issue for most work that you are likely to carry out. However, there are some circumstances that you should be aware of before beginning renovations.

restrictions

Most restrictions are applied to houses that are historic buildings and/or are in conservation areas, national parks, or areas of outstanding natural beauty. Houses in a community overseen by an association may also have restrictions. If your property fits into any of these categories,

always call the appropriate local authority before commencing any plans. However, even in these cases, formal permission is rarely required for interior alterations, minor improvements, and general repairs and maintenance. Projects that definitely require planning permission are generally those in which an area of the house has a "change of use," normally when business purposes are proposed. For example, if you wish to divide off a section of your home for business use, or you want to create a separate apartment. So in general, in addition to these restrictions, as long as the exterior appearance of the building is not changed, interior work may be carried out relatively free from too many planning obstacles. But, if in doubt about what is permissible, it is best to contact your local Department of Planning and Zoning.

Exterior work can often be subject to strict building restrictions. Always check with an appropriate body before embarking on work that may require authorization.

building regulations

While most interior renovation is unlikely to require actual planning permission, all construction work should adhere to building regulations. So whenever you plan to carry out any construction work, contact your Department of Planning and Zoning, who will be able to provide any necessary guidelines for potential work.

making a scale drawing

It is always sensible to make a scale drawing of a proposed construction job, in order to get a firm idea of material quantities. This does not have to be up to architectural standards, but it should provide enough detail to give you a good idea of the effect a project will have, and how it will change the existing look of your home. Graph paper always makes any technical drawing easier, and allows for more accurate measurement. It can often be helpful to add furniture to the diagram, so that you can gauge the effect of the alteration on the overall layout of the room—this can be especially important when dividing an existing room into two separate areas, as the amount of space is obviously reduced.

time

Always consider the time required to complete a project, as this can influence the most convenient time to commence the job. For example, while some projects can be completed in a weekend, other jobs will take longer, causing disruption to the household for several days. Most projects in this book are designed to be completed within a weekend, although the actual finishing may

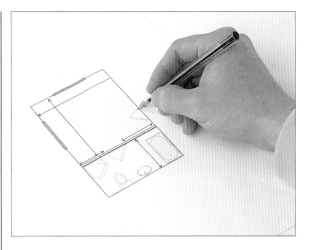

Making a scale drawing can help you to visualize the effect of any work on the surrounding environment. Adding furniture to the diagram will also help.

take longer. As soon as you begin to combine a number of projects or work on large areas, completing jobs can become more difficult. This is especially true of projects that run between weekends or evenings, so it is advisable either to break them down into smaller sections, which can be completed as part of an overall larger renovation, or take time off from day-to-day work in order to make headway into the particular task. Otherwise, pressure to finish the job and minimize disruption can lead to inadequate work with poor finishing. Never underestimate the time involved in a project, and consider it an important part of the planning procedure to decide on dates and times when the work can be done, and within what time it can be finished.

budgeting

The greatest expense in a construction project is usually the price of the labor itself, and therefore by reducing this input, costs are reduced. If professional trades are required, this should be given priority in terms of your overall budgeting strategy. Aside from this, material costs can be calculated relatively easily so long as accurate measurements are taken. Remember that bulk buying of particular materials should mean financial discounts, and it is always worth shopping around for the best deals. This is especially the case with common items such as general lumber and wallboard because the market is so competitive, and suppliers can vary their prices from week to week. If your planning is comprehensive, you have a better chance of remaining within your budget. However, it is always worth building in a slight surplus requirement to your figures so that if work does take longer—or requires more materials— you are able to complete the project without delay.

Many DIY tasks will cause some inevitable disruption to the household. Bear this in mind when planning a job, and aim to commence work at a time convenient to all of those involved.

dealing with professionals

Before starting any construction work, it is important to establish what work you are capable of doing yourself and to what extent you will need professional help. Small renovations or repairs are unlikely to require a great deal of assistance, but when tackling any major renovation, it is almost certain that the services of plumbers, electricians, or contractors will be required. In these cases, try to identify the kind of assistance you require and understand how to get the best service.

architects and surveyors

In some circumstances, it may be necessary to draw on the services of architects and surveyors. Although not considered conventional "craftsmen", they supply services that enable the practical side of major renovations to be planned and carried out in the correct manner. Architects really need to be employed only on larger projects where major design features have to be considered. On large projects, architects or surveyors can be employed in a kind of project management role, overseeing general work to ensure it meets building codes (see page 30). Bear in mind that these services are expensive and fees for monitoring work can add another 10 percent to the original cost of drawing plans. There may also be daily or hourly rate charges for site attendance.

Professional advice for major projects is always advisable, particularly for projects that may require building permits. Bear these costs in mind when planning the work.

finding good craftsmen

Finding good, reliable craftsmen can be difficult—there is no point in hiring the best bricklayer in the area if he never shows up for work. The best method is to use personal recommendations, as you can see or hear about the quality of the work from a former client. The other alternative is to contact three or four advertised companies for estimates. However, although this may help to ensure a competitive price, it does not guarantee the quality of the work or the reliability of the tradesperson. Even companies that display particular trade association medallions may be no more reliable than other advertisers, so check the credentials with the association itself and then with an independent body. Always ask to have a look at a person's work, preferably through the property owner and then perhaps with the builder or craftsman.

estimates, quotes, and prices

Before allowing any craftsman to begin work in your home, it is essential to know how much the actual job is going to cost. Estimates, quotes, and prices can be a minefield—and are frequently the source of customers' disgruntlement. The main factor to bear in mind at this stage is that if you receive an estimate or a quote, this is exactly the case—they are only estimates or quotes and therefore the price you pay can inflate considerably. If at all possible, it is best to get an exact price from the craftsman, which should not fluctuate unless you decide to change the specifications for the work. In some circumstances, an estimate may be necessary, as you may not have made final decisions on specifications and need to see how the project develops. However, the closer you can get to deciding on a price before the work begins, the better position you will find yourself in when budgeting for the job and keeping track of payments.

You will usually have to make an initial downpayment, especially if the craftsman is supplying expensive material, but generally speaking there is no reason to pay the full amount until the job is complete and you are happy with the

Keep the lines of communication open. Although the cost of work may rise slightly as the job progresses, this can be negotiated at each stage, helping you monitor the cost overall.

finished product. For long projects, it is fair to stage payments throughout the job, but always leave the largest payment until completion. Finally, treat contractors or craftsmen who insist on cash-only payments with some suspicion. Although there are potential savings to be made in this line, it means you have no recourse in terms of defective work or problems. Such methods of payment could also suggest illegal transactions in the eyes of the relevant tax authorities.

extras

On making any final payment, the words "extras", "extra work carried out", or "add-ons" on your bill can add a surprising amount to the figure you were expecting to pay. In many cases, these may be items that you authorized during the overall work. However, it is always best to get a price for extra work before it is done, so that shocks do not occur at the final stage of payment. Alternately, arrange during the initial contract stage that any extra work has to be carried out on your authority and is charged at a specific rate. This makes it much easier to keep a track of expenses and prevent unexpected surprises with the final statement.

avoiding disputes

Disputes can easily be avoided as long as you have a written contract. Over half the battle is won if you have chosen the right craftsman. Further gains can be made by ensuring that the price you are quoted is written and detailed in terms of the work to be carried out. This therefore acts as an accurate referral document for all parties. Aside from this, the only problems that generally arise concern the standard of work compared to what was initially agreed. Most of these problems can be sorted out through discussion and compromise, and it is best to avoid legal wrangles unless absolutely necessary. But, if you are that unhappy with the work carried out, your only option may be to withhold payment and hand the matter over to a lawyer.

In following these simple guidelines, you should be well equipped for employing the services of various craftsmen. Simply remember that, in all occupations, there are both good and bad operators and that the building business gets more than its fair share of criticism. However, if you do have a reliable craftsman at your disposal, pay them on time and recommend them to friends—in looking after their interests, you will almost certainly be looking after your own.

Professional craftsmen will do a good job for a fair price. However, before agreeing to the terms and conditions of the contract, establish the length of time and expense of the project.

altering the structure of a wall

The type and extent of work required to alter a wall structure will largely depend on the existing structure. Before deciding on the exact changes you would like to make, it is important to identify the kind of wall you currently have, so that you can gauge the best procedures for transformation. As always, the key issue is whether the wall is load-bearing or non-load-bearing—only once this has been established can planning begin for alteration. This chapter covers a range of projects, some with more structural implications than others, but many of the outlined tasks deal with the more aesthetic intentions of altering the structure of walls within your home.

Open-plan dining and living areas create
a very relaxed and comfortable feel to
your home and surroundings.

safety at work

Safety is always of paramount importance when considering any aspect of home improvement. Aside from general working tools, it is necessary to build up a collection of safety equipment, so that you are adequately protected when carrying out any task around the home. When choosing safety equipment, never compromise on quality and be sure that the articles you purchase display the relevant safety standard markings.

first-aid kit

By far the greatest number of injuries resulting from home improvement are very minor cuts and abrasions, and therefore it is essential to have a well stocked first aid kit in your home.

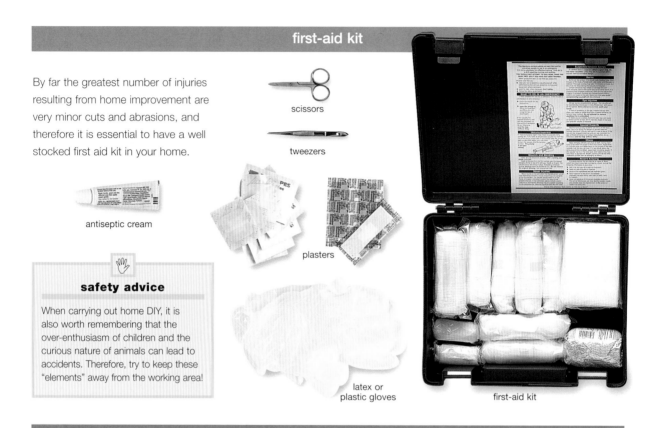

scissors

tweezers

antiseptic cream

plasters

latex or plastic gloves

first-aid kit

safety advice

When carrying out home DIY, it is also worth remembering that the over-enthusiasm of children and the curious nature of animals can lead to accidents. Therefore, try to keep these "elements" away from the working area!

safety equipment

A range of safety equipment is available for various DIY tasks. Some items are intended for particular jobs, but many pieces, such as work boots, goggles, and protective gloves, should be worn in most situations.

dust mask

protective gloves

knee pads

lead test kit

respirator mask

hard hat

goggles

ear protectors

work boots

Gaining easy access to all areas of a room is an important part of safety rules. Never risk injury by overstretching or overreaching—instead use ladders or scaffolding so that you can reach all the areas in a room with ease. This is especially the case for exterior work, where tower scaffolding or mechanical platforms may be a practical option. This kind of equipment can be rented and helps to provide a safe working environment, plus it saves time when extensive, high level work is needed.

ladders

Ladders are the most commonly used and versatile of access equipment options. However, despite their simple construction and ease of use, there are a number of simple but important rules to obey when using them.

- Be sure that the distance between the base of the ladder and the wall is one-quarter the distance between the base of the wall and top of the ladder.
- Ensure that the base of the ladder is on a level, nonslip surface.
- Ensure that the top of the ladder

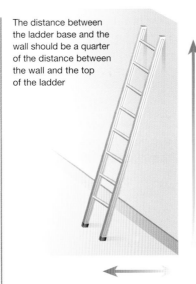

The distance between the ladder base and the wall should be a quarter of the distance between the wall and the top of the ladder

Careful ladder positioning is vital for the safety of its user.

has total contact with the wall surface.
- Ensure that all rungs are secure and have not been damaged in any way.
- When working outside, take care to avoid overhead powerlines.

Multipurpose ladders are usually constructed from aluminium and can be used as stepladders, extra-long traditional ladders, and even as a working platform like the one below. However, such versatility means that you must check use guidelines carefully as joint locking systems can vary.

a simple working platform

Adjustable trestles allow their height to be changed for the particular job at hand

Ensure the trestles are spaced every 60in (1.5m)

Position trestles at intervals below the scaffold planks

Ensure that all trestle feet are touching the ground

GENERAL TOOL CARE

Accidents can often be caused by tools that have either been poorly maintained or are so old that they are no longer safe to use. Careful tool maintenance will always ensure that you get the best out of your tools and that they are safe to use. Below are a few points to consider regarding tool maintenance and safety.

- Chisels, planes, and cutting equipment must always be kept as sharp as possible. More accidents are caused by blunt tools slipping on the surface than by sharp tools. An oilstone is ideal to keep tools such as chisels razor sharp.

- Electric cables and wires on power tools can break or crack, so they should be inspected regularly to ensure they are in good condition. Power tools in general may also require periodic servicing. Power-tool efficiency can also be hampered by the accessories you use with them. Therefore bits and blades should be replaced when necessary, as old ones can strain the motor of the power tool being used.

- Hammers can often slip off the head of a nail when you are attempting to hammer it in. To avoid this, sand the striking face of the hammer with fine-grade sandpaper in order to clean it and provide a fine key. It is surprising what a difference this simple procedure can make. This may be applied to all types of hammers, except a milled face hammer, and is useful for any hammering procedure.

recognizing problems—1

Cracks and faults in wall and ceiling surfaces can often look more problematic than they actually are. However, while the main concern may appear to be aesthetic, cracks should also be seen as signs of potential structural problems—such as movement—so it is important to try to determine their cause. Many cracks form for particular reasons and can easily be identified and categorized. The diagram below shows common areas where cracking occurs.

testing cracks and movement

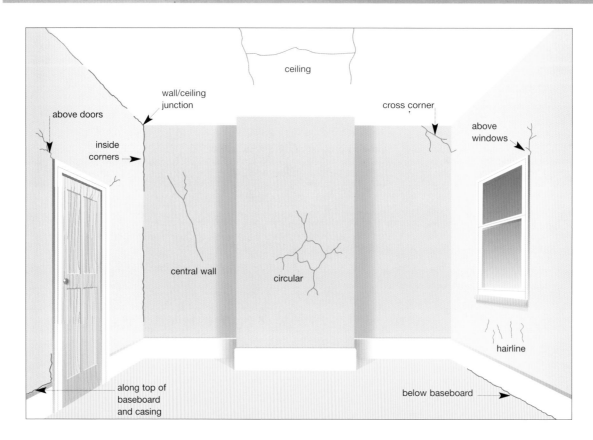

ceiling

wall/ceiling junction

cross corner

above doors

above windows

inside corners

central wall

circular

hairline

along top of baseboard and casing

below baseboard

Determining the movement and development of cracks—if any—can obviously be difficult. Such movements tend to be slight and take time to develop, making it virtually impossible to monitor accurately. For this reason, crack monitoring systems can now be bought that enable accurate measuring of any movement. Although manufacturers' guidelines do vary, the general principles for use remain the same for most commercial brands. If in doubt, contact the product manufacturer or a structural surveyor for further assistance.

1 Screw the detector in place, with the detection scale roughly positioned over the crack. Do not overtighten the screws at this stage.

2 Shift the scale on the detector so that it sits precisely in line with the crack. Tighten the screws when you are happy with the position.

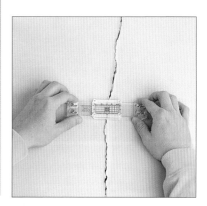

3 Remove the plastic lugs from the edge of the detector to free the two-plate mechanism. If movement occurs, the scale on one plate will move in relation to the other, thereby making it possible to observe accurately the extent and duration of any movement. Detectors, of slightly varying designs, can also be used across corners or at ceiling and floor level.

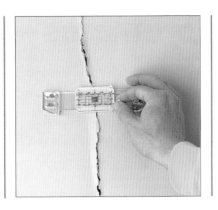

safety advice

Always seek professional advice about cracks that may represent structural problems. Detecting subsidence or structural faults is a skilled profession, and should never be underestimated. Failure to gauge the gravity of the situation could present long-term dangers to both the structure of the house and the health of its inhabitants.

type	causes of cracks & remedies
internal corners	These cracks are often a result of settlement in new homes and therefore can be filled and painted. Persistent cracking should be monitored.
ceiling	Ceiling cracks that are very directional, in that they have a relatively straight course or turn at right angles, tend to result from slight board movement in the ceiling structure. These can be filled and painted or, if they persist, taping can normally prevent them from reappearing.
cross corner	Cracks that extend across a corner from one wall to another can represent a subsidence problem, especially if lines of brick or block work can be picked out. In such cases, seek professional advice.
above windows	Cracks are often visible extending from the corners of windows up toward ceiling level. So long as they are relatively small, they generally represent slight settlement or movement. However, large cracks that show a vertical shift should be investigated further.
hairline	These cracks are common, multidirectional, and suggest slight movement of a plaster surface. Numbers tend to increase with the age of the building. Most are superficial and do not represent any cause for alarm. However, if new plaster surfaces display a number of persistent cracks, this could suggest that the plaster was poorly mixed or has not bonded correctly to the wall. In such cases, replastering may be necessary.
below baseboard	Gaps below baseboard tend to suggest that the baseboard was poorly installed. However, cracks that continue to develop could reflect floor problems or some subsidence. Those that continue to grow should be investigated by a professional.
circular	Cracks that form irregular, circular shapes tend to reflect areas of plaster delaminating from the wall lath or substrate. This is common in old lath-and-plaster walls, where age has taken its toll and the plaster surface has become unstable in localized areas. The affected area can be removed and patch-plastered.
central wall cracks	These may occur for any number of reasons and should simply be monitored to check that they do not grow wider. Seek professional advice in extreme cases.
along top of baseboard and casing	Cracks occur in these places either because of age and slight building movement or because the materials are new and take a little time to settle to the atmospheric conditions of the particular room environment. Unless the cracks persist or grow after filling and repainting, there is generally no cause for alarm.
above doors	See explanation for cracks above windows.
wall/ceiling junction	These cracks commonly occur during settlement in new houses, and as a result of age in older ones. Small cracks can be filled and redecorated, whereas larger types should be monitored to check that they do not expand, thus requiring structural repair.

recognizing problems—2

In addition to movement, structural areas of the home can also be affected by moisture and insect or fungal infestation. Many such problems are easily remedied, but others can have wider consequences and be extremely damaging to the building structure, especially if they are left untreated. These sorts of problems can take many forms and affect different areas of the home, but the diagram below outlines many of the key areas to look out for.

moisture and infestation

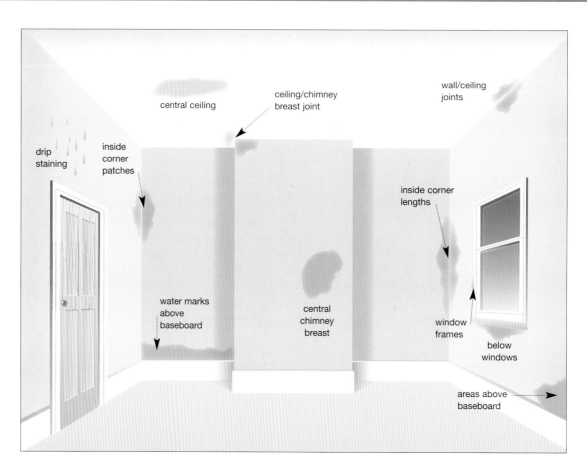

- central ceiling
- ceiling/chimney breast joint
- wall/ceiling joints
- drip staining
- inside corner patches
- inside corner lengths
- water marks above baseboard
- central chimney breast
- window frames
- below windows
- areas above baseboard

other problems of infestation

Aside from those problems usually associated with moisture, there are other potential problems that can be linked to insects and fungal attack.

dry rot

This is an exceptionally damaging form of decay that mainly affects wood but also spreads across masonry. While identifying and counteracting the source will remedy the problem, dry rot attacks with actual fungicidal spores that spread the disease very quickly, making it difficult to eradicate. Dry rot does initially take hold in areas of damp and poor ventilation. It is identified by thin, white strands that spread along surfaces, rather like a spider's web. The effect breaks down building structure irreparably. Treatment should therefore be fast, involving the cutting out and destroying of all infected areas. New wood and materials should be treated to protect them against dry rot infection.

woodworm

These are basically the larvae of particular beetles, and so there are two methods for discovering if you have the problem. Either the appearance of the beetles provides evidence of their presence, or more commonly, the actual flight holes are visible, indicating their existence in the household woodwork. Action against woodworm must be swift as the parasite can quickly break down wood and spread throughout the entire house. Spray infected areas with the appropriate insecticide and also any unaffected woodwork that is nearby, to prevent further spreading. When replacing any wood, always make sure that the new material has been preserved properly. If in any doubt, seek professional advice.

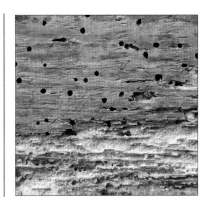

type	causes of damp & remedies
central ceiling	These patches tend to be a result of leaking pipes in the ceiling, or at top floor level they may be a roof leak dripping on to surfaces below. Consult a plumber for fastening pipework, and make any necessary shingle repair work at roof level.
ceiling/chimney breast joint	Damp patches that develop in these areas may be a result of a gap in flashing around the chimney. Therefore inspect the area and effect a repair if required.
wall/ceiling joints	At top floor level, this is often a result of a blocked gutter. Unblock the gutter to eliminate the resulting damp penetration. This sort of damp may also result from a lean-to building, where the flashing at the point where it joins the main building has deteriorated. Check the flashing and repair if necessary.
inside corner lengths	Elongated damp patches along inside corners often indicate a blocked or cracked downpipe on the exterior of the building. Dripping water therefore gradually penetrates, causing a persistent damp wall stain. Unblock or replace the downpipe as required.
window frames	Damp penetration is common around the edges of windows due to a buildup of condensation or because of a break in the seal around the edge of the window frame itself. Check that the window is sealed correctly and reapply silicone sealant if necessary. If the problem is condensation-based, install better ventilation systems for the room or simply open windows more often.
below windows	Seals beneath windows may be damaged or the drip guard below the sill may be blocked. Check both areas and clear or reseal as required.
areas above baseboard	Large damp patches above baseboard are often a result of the buildup of material, such as piles of soil, on the exterior side of the wall surface. This bridges the foundation coating and causes moisture penetration. Simply remove the obstructive material, and ensure soil levels are kept below the foundation coating level.
central chimney breast	These patches commonly develop in unused chimneys where the chimney and fireplace have been blocked off. The unused chimney void therefore has no ventilation, causing the moist, damp air to penetrate through the chimney breast. To cure this problem, install an air vent in the chimney breast in order to improve air flow and circulation.
water marks above baseboard	If these are not a result of the foundation coating being bridged on the other side of the wall, then it may be straightforward rising damp. This is common in older houses with no foundation coating or in houses where the coating is damaged and therefore allowing water penetration. Various dampproofing injection systems are the most effective cure. These systems are always best carried out by professionals.
inside corner patches	Small damp patches in walls often result from patches of damaged pointing or base coat on the exterior of the building. Simple repair of the appropriate material should cure the problem.
drip staining	Visible stains from drips or running moisture on the walls tends to point in the direction of a condensation problem. This commonly occurs in kitchens and bathrooms. Simply install better ventilation systems and open windows more often.

removing a load-bearing wall ⁄⁄⁄⁄

Removing a load-bearing wall is not a project that should be undertaken lightly, and professional advice and instruction should be sought before carrying out this procedure. Total wall removal is rare, and it is more common to remove a load-bearing wall in order to open up the floor layout and convert two rooms into a single area with a more open-plan design. The work involved is strongly based around supportive measures.

The most important factor when taking on work of this kind is to ensure that there is adequate support, both while the area of wall is being removed and when the work is complete. Whether removing a masonry wall (shown here) or a wood-framed wall, you must set up a temporary support to hold the weight of the ceiling during demolition.

It is also crucial to install a lintel or a header for permanent support. The size and makeup of this support beam depends upon the structure of the wall you are removing and the span of the opening you need to make. Both these factors require serious calculation, and the beam type and construction should be decided in

consultation with a structural engineer. Once these precautions, procedures, and planning have been finalized, the work itself is manageable. First the opening must be made, and second, the supportive beam must be inserted. In a masonry wall (shown here), a steel I-beam serves as the lintel. In a wood-framed wall, a header is used.

making the opening

Preparation and planning is essential for this procedure, and because the nature of the work is relatively demanding in a physical sense, two or more

people are much better than one in this instance. Also keep the work area clear of any obstacles as much as possible, as this will help to reduce the likelihood of accidents.

1 Mark out the size of the opening on the wall surface

2 Knock holes through the wall above the proposed opening

3 Insert needle braces through the holes

4 Support the needle braces with bearing posts on both sides of the wall

5 Use a stone cutter or hand sledge and brick chisel to cut around the edge of the opening

6 Remove the blocks or bricks by first loosening with a hand sledge and brick chisel and then levering out with a pry bar or lifting by hand

7 Continue to remove blocks until the entire area is clear

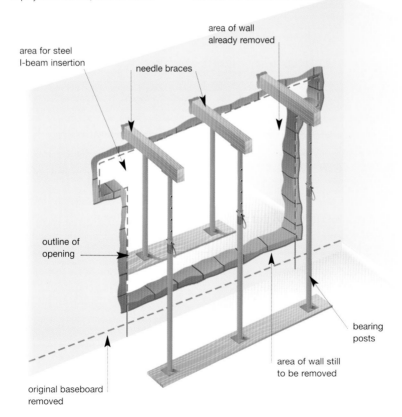

area of wall already removed

area for steel I-beam insertion

needle braces

outline of opening

original baseboard removed

bearing posts

area of wall still to be removed

Two or more people will definitely be required for this stage of the project as even the smallest lintels are surprisingly heavy. It is also a time-consuming process when setting the I-beam in position. Make sure that you check the level of the I-beam because problems will be difficult to rectify later.

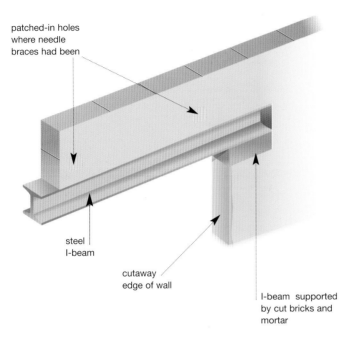

patched-in holes where needle braces had been

steel I-beam

cutaway edge of wall

I-beam supported by cut bricks and mortar

1 At the top corners of the opening, take out bricks or blocks to accommodate the I-beam ends

2 Check and recheck measurements to ensure that the lintel will fit into the required space

3 Apply a bed of mortar to this area before lifting the I-beam into place

4 Check that the I-beam is level. Use cut bricks or blocks, wedged beneath the end of the I-beam, to rectify if necessary

5 Apply more mortar around the I-beam ends to ensure it will be held securely in place

6 Frame around the I-beam to allow for drywall to be installed

7 Remove needle braces and patch in holes

factors to consider

In addition to the practical considerations of how to support your wall, there are also a number of other issues that should be carefully addressed.

needle brace requirement

The number of needle braces that you will require for the support will depend on the width of the opening that you plan to create. The actual needle brace dimensions should not be less than 4 x 6in (10 x 15cm), but you should consult a structural engineer in order to establish the exact needle brace requirements of your wall.

bearing

Steel bearing posts can be rented at a relatively low cost, and their adjustable nature makes them ideal for these supporting purposes. Make sure that the bases of the posts are positioned on scaffold planks so that the weight distribution is evened out. Most post bases have nail holes so that they can be nailed into the scaffold planks to eliminate any risk of them moving.

I-beam support

In many cases the new lintel may be accommodated in the existing wall structure with no extra support below it. However, in some cases it may be necessary to install extra concrete support. Consult a structural engineer for the correct requirements in your particular circumstances.

safety equipment

This sort of work requires close attention to safety and all the necessary precautions must be taken. Wear protective gloves, goggles, and a hard hat when taking down the wall. A dust mask may also be needed, especially when clearing away the rubble and dust caused by wall removal. The area must be kept as clear as possible from obstructions, and rubble should be removed regularly. (See page 36 for more safety advice and page 12 for lead and asbestos precautions.)

removing a non-load-bearing wall ⚒⚒

Before embarking on this project it is vital to ensure that the wall is definitely non-load-bearing. Once this is established, removal requires little more than a simple methodical approach. However, it is important to bear in mind that there will undoubtedly be a certain amount of repair and cleaning up to do once the wall is gone, so try to minimize the amount of damage caused to the ceiling and other wall surfaces when you remove the wall.

The techniques required for removing a non-load-bearing wall will largely depend on whether the wall is of a stud construction or built from solid bricks or blocks. Once this has been established, ensure that electrical outlets, switches, and plumbing have been removed and rerouted as necessary by an electrician or plumber.

tips of the trade

Never underestimate the amount of mess and dust that can be generated by projects such as wall removal. Plan the task to fit in conveniently with your busy household (such as on a weekend, when disruption will not be a problem) and take the time to remove all furniture and floorcoverings from the room(s) in which you will be working.

removing a stud wall

The lightweight construction of stud walls means that their removal tends to be a fairly straightforward job, as long as you follow an organized, basic order of work.

tools for the job

pry bar or crowbar

stud finder

hand saw

1 Begin by removing any features on the wall surface such as picture rails, cove, and baseboards. A pry bar or crowbar is the ideal tool to pry

baseboard away from the wall. Try not to damage the baseboard as it can possibly be reused on another wall.

2 Locate a central stud in the wall, either by using a stud finder or by tapping along the wall surface with the head of the pry bar—areas between studs will sound hollow, whereas stud positions will make the noise of a dull thud. Dig into the wall

by the stud with the end of the bar and lever the drywall away from the stud framework.

3 When all the drywall has been removed, begin to take out the wooden studs by sawing through

each one in a suitable place. Cut slightly above the plate or firestops —if you cut too tight to the joint, the saw may catch the nails or screws in the studs.

4 To remove the floor plate, it is often easier to saw it into separate sections. This helps to reduce its bonding power with the floor surface.

safety advice

Wear gloves, goggles, a dust mask, and a hard hat to protect yourself from flying debris or sharp edges. See page 12 for lead and asbestos precautions.

Use the pry bar to lever the
sections of the plate away from
the floor surface. A similar technique
may be used for the ceiling plate and
wall plates as required.

part removal of a solid block wall

Non-load-bearing block or brick walls
may be totally or partially removed
to create a larger room space.
Partial removal can provide a more
aesthetically pleasing finish because,
instead of producing a completely
open room, it creates two areas
with character and interest.

tools for the job

pencil or chalk line
pry bar
hand sledge
brick chisel
corner bead
hacksaw
plastering trowel
level

Removal of blocks can be harder
work than that of a simple stud wall,
and you will need additional tools
such as a hand sledge and brick
chisel to break down the joints. It is
always best to start at the top and
work down, removing single blocks if
possible. When partially removing a
wall, draw guidelines directly on the

wall surface using a chalk line or
pencil and level. A stone cutter can be
used to make an accurate cut down
these guidelines, but in most cases it
is easy enough to follow the line using
the hand sledge and brick chisel.

1 Once the main area of wall has
been removed, straighten up the
block edges as much as possible,
and remove any loose mortar.

2 Use a hacksaw (see page 133)
to cut some corner bead to the
required height of the wall edge and
position it along the edge using
bonding plaster to hold it in place.
It may be necessary to use a torpedo
level in order to gain a truly plumb
position for the bead. Position another
corner bead on the adjacent edge.
Hold the beads in position while the
bonding plaster dries.

3 Apply bonding agent to the
edges of the trimmed blocks.
Make sure that you work the solution
into every crevice and allow it to dry
to a tacky consistency.

4 Then apply more bonding
plaster along the entire wall
edge. A perfect finish is not required
at this stage, so just ensure a good
coverage of the whole edge. Score
the bonding plaster (see page 130)
before allowing it to dry.

5 Mix and apply finishing plaster
over the bonding coat, creating
a smooth, flat finish. Use the rigid
frame of the corner beads on which
to rest the edges of the plastering
trowel so that the finish is flush.
Apply plaster along the adjacent
edges of the corner bead, feathering
it with the original wall.

aligning floors ⚒

Once a wall has been removed—whether totally or partially—it can be common for the floors between what were once two rooms to vary slightly in level. This happens most often in older houses, where either there has been some slight subsidence or an addition has been built with slightly different floor levels to those of the original house. The reasons for variation in levels is not that important, but correcting the situation is vital in order to obtain a suitable floor joint.

Even when floor levels are similar, it is likely that you may need to fill the gap left by the old wall. This is often the case when a block wall has been removed either the blocks break off at ground level, producing a rough surface, or the blocks drop below the floor level, leaving a gap to fill between the two rooms. The techniques required for such tasks will be mainly dependent on whether the floors are concrete- or wood-framed.

concrete floors

tools for the job

dust brush

brick chisel

hand sledge

paintbrush

gauging trowel

wooden batten

plastering trowel

After removing a stud wall, little repair is normally required because the wall would have been built on top of an existing concrete screed. However, when removing a block wall, it can be common to find that the concrete screed was laid after the block wall was erected. This means the block removal either leaves a large hole along the line of what was the wall base, or the blocks are broken away leaving a rough, unfinished joint across the floor. In either situation, some repair work will be required.

1 Dust away as much debris and loose material as possible from the old block wall base. Ensure that none of the broken block edges protrude above the surrounding floor surface. Trim such protrusions using a brick chisel and hand sledge.

2 Apply a bonding agent generously along the entire broken block joint, allowing the solution to overlap the edges of the concrete screed on both sides of the joint.

3 Mix up some mortar (5 parts building sand to 1 part cement) and press it firmly into the joint. Use the edge of a gauging trowel to

"chop" the mortar in, thus ensuring it gets into every area along the length of the joint. Allow the mortar to protrude slightly above the surrounding concrete.

4 Cut a length of batten, slightly longer than the width of the joint, and position it across the joint. Slowly push it along the length of the joint move the batten in a side-to-side sawing motion so that it gradually removes the excess mortar to create a flush joint between the existing

screed and the new mortar. This process may need to be repeated two or three times to produce a finish that is totally smooth and flat.

Once dry, mix up some self-levelling compound and apply it along the joint, allowing a large overlap on to the surrounding screed. Gently spread the compound using a plastering trowel. Allow it to settle and dry, providing a perfectly smooth and level joint.

making a slope

Where floor levels vary slightly, a slope or step may need to be constructed. Slopes can be created by simply feathering the edges of the self-levelling compound to produce an even drop between the two levels. Alternatively, the floors can be evened by applying a greater depth of compound to the entire surface of the lower concrete screed level.

wooden floors

tools for the job

cordless drill/driver

claw hammer

pry bar

One of the key considerations when working on a wooden floor is whether the surface will be exposed thus making aesthetic considerations important. If it is to be covered, a firm, level joint is the only major concern, but exposed floors need more care.

repairing a covered floor

Attach lengths of 1 x 2in (2.5 x 5cm) batten to the wooden joists on either side of the old wall joint. Ensure that the top edge of each batten sits directly flush with the top of the joist and therefore precisely below the subfloor or flooring.

Filling the gap will depend on its dimensions. Ideally, nail a new floorboard in position along the joint, allowing the nails to go through the board and into the battens that have been attached to the joists. Different gap dimensions may require you to cut a board such as particle board to the appropriate size before nailing it in position along the gap.

repairing an exposed floor

Most exposed floors are made up of traditional floorboards, so filling gaps may also entail adjusting the original board position.

Attach lengths of 1 x 2in (2.5 x 5cm) batten to the wooden joist on the floorboard side of the old wall joint. Use a pry bar to lift every other board carefully along the joint junction. (You can use the same tool to lift sheets of particle board flooring.) Alternately, the boards may need to be unscrewed.

Use a claw hammer to remove any old nails that are protruding from the floor joists.

Cut boards to length and use them to infill across the floor surface, creating a neat finish.

building a stud wall—1 ⤻⤻⤻

Stud walls are built in two main stages, and the following four pages explain each step. Before any work can begin, however, you must first establish the direction of the ceiling and floor joists—this will determine whether the top and sole plates are to run parallel or at right angles to them. Use a stud finder or density detector for this task. These simple tools contain sensor pads that trigger a light every time they pass over a joist.

When the wall runs parallel to the joists, it is best to position the sole plate directly above a joist and the top plate below a joist. On second floors, an additional joist below floor level should be used to provide extra strength (see page 13). When the wall is to run at right angles to the joists there is greater flexibility because attachments will be made on subsequent joists across the span of the room. So be prepared to find a compromise between your desired position for the wall and the most practical location.

making the frame

tools for the job

stud finder
hammer
chalk line
level
pencil
hand saw
cordless drill
tape measure
board lifter (optional)
plumb bob (optional)

Studs may either be 2 x 4in (5 x 10cm), 2 x 6in (5 x 15cm), or 2 x 3in (5 x 7.5cm) in dimension, and are generally made from sawn softwood. Traditionalists choose sturdy, thicker studs whereas most modern buildings will contain the smaller ones. The distance between the studs is vital—if you are covering the frame with drywall that is ½in (12.5mm) thick, the studs

must be a minimum of 16in (40cm) and a maximum of 24in (60cm) apart; if you are using ⅝in (16mm) drywall, the studs should be 24in (60cm) apart.

1 Use a stud finder to trace the position of joists and any wiring or plumbing above the ceiling surface.

2 Having decided on the wall position, hammer a nail into the ceiling close to the wall joint, at what will be the center of the top plate position. Do the same at the opposite ceiling/wall joint.

3 Attach a chalk line between the two nails and snap a guideline onto the ceiling surface. This line will

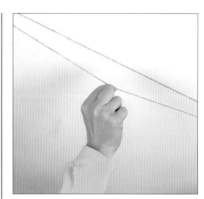

help to provide the exact position for the top plate.

4 Use a level and pencil to continue this guideline down both walls at each end of the ceiling guideline. Continue the lines down to floor level.

5 Hold a stud section at baseboard level and direct the wall pencil guideline so that it bisects the stud. Make a pencil guideline on either side of the stud, thus marking the baseboard. Remove the stud and cut out this section of baseboard in order to accommodate the sole plate. Repeat this process on the opposite wall. The guidelines should now indicate the position of

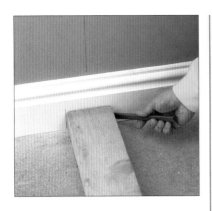

the top plate (ceiling), sole plate (floor), and wall plates.

6 Cut a stud to the exact length between the opposing walls. Position it, allowing the cut baseboard sections to accommodate each end of the plate length. Mark on this piece of plate (the sole plate), the exact position of any doors that may be required. Remember to allow for the door jamb and shimming space.

7 Nail or screw the sole plate into the floor at 16in (40cm) intervals. For concrete floors, drill and plug the holes first.

8 Cut a plate to the exact length between the opposing walls at ceiling level, and make a pencil mark bisecting the center of the joists at each end. Align the plate with the snapped ceiling line, then screw the plate to each joist crossing.

9 Cut two studs to the exact length between the top and sole plate on each wall. Crown the studs, pointing their natural curves in the same direction, and fasten them in place.

10 Mark off the sole plate at 16in (40cm) intervals in order to indicate the positions

for the vertical studs. If a door position has been marked, skip any studs that fall in the doorway but continue marking at the same intervals.

11 Cut small blocks of wood and nail them in position at the side of each stud guideline. This will help to make fastening the vertical studs in place easier. The frame is now complete and ready to be filled in (see page 50 for the next stage).

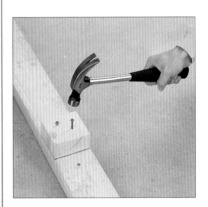

USING A PLUMB BOB

It is also possible to create guidelines using a plumb bob or line. Once you have established the ceiling guideline (steps 1–2), attach the plumb bob to each of the nails in turn and mark along, and at the bottom of, the line to gain a vertical guide. The plumb bob may also be used from a central ceiling position to mark sole plate guidelines along the floor. Be sure that the plumb bob is stationary and not touching anything before marking off.

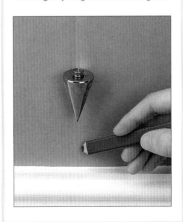

building a stud wall—2 ⚏⚏⚏

Once the outer framework of the stud wall has been installed, attention can be turned to filling in the framework and drywalling. Make a final check on the plumbness of the frame and its positioning, because any slight adjustments are best made at this stage rather than later. See page 48 for a list of tool requirements.

studding the frame

1 Measure each stud and cut the required lengths. Fasten them at the base, holding them against the block supports to prevent them from moving. Use sinker nails and toenail them in at an angle on both sides of the stud, so that the nails penetrate into the sole plate.

2 With the stud fastened at its base, hold a level against the length in order to find the precise

vertical fastening position in the top plate. Drive toenails into each side of the stud and into the top plate.

3 Keep checking the level and adjusting the stud until it is precisely vertical, before securing it in place.

4 To make the door frame, cut a header to the exact size between the two studs on either side of the door opening. Remember to check the correct height measurement for the door (including the door jamb), and nail the length in place, ensuring that it is level.

5 To add strength, install cripple studs vertically between the door head and top plate on the stud layout lines. Nails may be inserted in the base of the vertical stud, whereas at ceiling level, the nails must be angled through the vertical length into the top plate.

6 Blocking can be added between the studs in order to provide extra rigidity. These blocks should be positioned half way between the sole and top plates. Secure them in place with nails.

7 On completion of the framework, work on providing access for any services or electrical cables that may need to run through the wall. Drill holes through studs and blocks as required.

⑧ Thread cables through the holes drilled in the studs. (Check with a qualified electrician for the exact wiring requirements for the services you require.)

attaching the drywall

As discussed on page 48, ensure that you are using the correct thickness of drywall for the spacing of the studs. Bear in mind that if you are planning to use joint compound, the drywall should also have tapered edges (see page 84).

Invariably, sheets of drywall need to be cut to fit, so careful measuring is required. As most ceilings and wall surfaces are neither perfectly flat nor completely square, the edge of the sheets will often need to be "scribed" in order to produce a precise fit. This is most important at ceiling level and in corners because the joint needs to be as tight as possible (leaving a gap of no more than ⅛in/2.5mm), whereas at floor level there is some leeway because the baseboard will cover the joint.

tips of the trade

Although it is often easier and more practical to have two people hanging or installing drywall, it can be achieved working on your own with the aid of a drywall "T". This allows you to lever drywall sheets into position on the wall surface, while leaving your hands free for fastening purposes.

① Holding the sheet as close to the ceiling as possible (so that it touches), slide a small wooden block and pencil along the sheet, keeping the block resting against the ceiling surface. The pencil guideline produced will mimic the profile of the ceiling, providing a guideline to cut the drywall for the perfect fit.

② Use drywall nails or screws to fasten the sheets in place. Fastenings should be made between ½in (12mm) and 1in (25mm) from the board edges and at 6in (15cm) intervals or centers along all edges and studs. Fasten drywall around a door opening so that the joint is above the center of the door.

Although this is technically more difficult to measure and cut, after taping or finishing, a central board joint such as this will be less likely to crack than joints that run vertical from the door opening corners.

③ When one side of the wall is completely covered, drill the necessary holes in the drywall for

any electrical cables. Then, before drywalling the other side of the stud wall, install insulation blankets between all the studs. This is only necessary for exterior application or sound deadening. Finally, finish the drywall (see page 84) and trim the door opening.

tips of the trade

● **Blocking**—Install extra blocking between studs where heavy items are to be mounted on the wall surface. For example, ensure that an extra block is positioned to accommodate sinks or basins.

● **Flush joints**—When positioning all the studs and blocks, take extra care to ensure that the surfaces of all the particular joints are flush. Uneven joints may cause bows in the drywall, making installation difficult and causing weak spots.

● **Secure nailing**—When installing fasteners or nails, ensure that their heads sit slightly below surface level for a secure fastening, but not so far that the head of the nail causes the drywall to crumble and reduces the strength of the installation.

● **Screwing alternative**—Drywall screws instead of nails can be used to fasten sheeting. This can often be easier when working on your own and reduces the risk of damaging drywall with hammer blows.

● **Marking off**—It can be difficult to locate the exact position of studs when drywalling, as the wallboard itself is covering them. So when the stud framework has been completed, mark off where the center of each stud is located on the floor with a pencil. Then use a level to draw a pencil guideline on each board from floor to ceiling as you work.

making an arch ⁄⁄⁄⁄

Arches can be used as an alternative to traditional doors or square openings, adding greater character and providing a feature between rooms. Previously, such tasks involved a highly skilled procedure both to produce a framework for the arch and to finish off the surface with plaster. However, the manufacturing of arch forms has made the whole process much easier and faster for DIY enthusiasts.

making an arch in a stud wall

tools for the job

cordless drill/driver

screwdriver

tape measure

hacksaw

hammer

filling knife

plastering trowel

Although arches may be added to existing wall openings, starting from scratch and building them into a new stud wall is much easier. This is because a new wall, if constructed correctly, is more likely to be "true" and "square" compared to older walls.

1 Most forms will have pre-drilled holes to accommodate fasteners. Hold the form in position while drilling four pilot holes into the timber studs. Make sure that the front lip of the arch is level with the plasterboard on either side.

2 Secure the form in place with wood screws. Use a screwdriver rather than a cordless drill/driver to tighten the screws, as overtightening could crack the plaster form. Greater control of movement can be achieved by using a simple hand tool in situations like this.

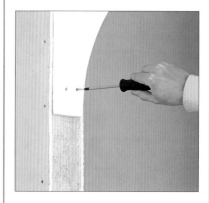

3 Measure and cut a piece of plasterboard to fit between the edge of the arch form and the floor for each side of the entrance. This is both to cover the wooden stud beneath, and to bring the surface up to the same depth as that created by the form. Fix the plasterboard in position with plasterboard nails, taking care not to damage the surface.

4 Cut corner bead to the correct length (form base to floor) and attach it on both edges of the opening. Fasten the corner bead in position using plasterboard nails. Remember to ensure that the apex of each corner bead aligns precisely with the respective bottom corners of the arch form.

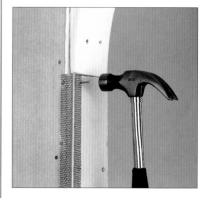

5 Repeat steps 1–4 to fit the second form and entrance lining around the arch. It is rare that the forms will join exactly—almost certainly gaps will occur between the top edges of the forms. To solve this, simply cut plaster sheeting to the appropriate shape and size and fix into position. Again, use corner bead to complete the edges.

👍 tips of the trade

Where the smooth form face meets the plastered edge of the entrance, it may be necessary to "feather" the joint with some joint compound in order to obtain a perfectly smooth arch. Once filled, use a fine-grit sandpaper to finish the joint.

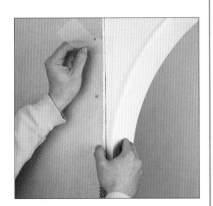

6 When the forms, plasterboard lining, and corner beads have all been positioned and aligned, fill the arch form holes with joint compound.

7 Tape the joints between the pieces of plasterboard, and between the board and the arches, with self-adhesive joint tape.

8 Apply plaster to the walls in the usual way (see pages 86–7), extending the plaster over and onto the arches. The actual arched face of the arches may not require plastering—this will depend upon the

type of form you have used. Once the plaster has been "polished" and then left to dry, the arch is ready for painting. With some forms, it may be necessary to apply two coats of plaster. This will depend on the depth of the form face in relation to the surrounding wall area. If the depth difference is more than ⅛in (2–3mm), apply two thin layers of plaster, rather than one thick coat.

Arches add shape to rooms and soften edges, producing a relaxed and comfortable atmosphere linking the decoration between two living areas.

pass-throughs ⁄⁄⁄

Pass-throughs provide ideal access for serving food from a kitchen into a dining area. Although they are still used for this purpose in many cases, they can also make attractive decorative features and may be constructed in a range of different styles. Building a pass-through in a solid block wall or a load-bearing wall will require greater effort (see opposite page). However, carrying out such a project in a non-load-bearing wall is a very straightforward exercise.

pass-through in a non-load-bearing stud wall

tools for the job

stud finder
pencil
torpedo level
tape measure
drywall saw
panel saw
hammer
cordless drill/driver
miter box or miter saw

1 Work out your preferred position for the pass-through, then use a stud finder to locate stud positions in the wall and to check for services such as wiring and plumbing. Be prepared to make some small adjustments according to the position of the wall studs and these services. (It is almost certain that you will need to cut through some studs, but try to adjust your measurements so that the sides of the opening correspond with the edges of the studs.)

2 Use a pencil and torpedo level to draw a guideline on the wall to show the exact size of the opening. It is essential to get dimensions and measurements as plumb and level as possible at this stage—this will help to make constructing the pass-through easier when the necessary hole has been made.

3 Use a drywall saw (see the lead and asbestos warning on page 12) to cut around the pencil outline. (This saw's sharp point pierces the plasterboard or drywall panels easily.) If you come across a stud obstruction, use the very end of the saw to plunge into the panel. Once the panel has been cut

around, it may be removed and discarded. Repeat the procedure for the other side of the wall. If the wall was insulated, cut the exposed insulation with a utility knife and remove it.

4 Remove blocking by first sawing through it with the panel saw. Then lever out the blocks with a pry bar or hammer. If you try to saw too closely to the vertical stud, it is likely that you will come into contact with nails or screw fasteners and damage the saw blade. Instead, remove such fasteners with a hacksaw.

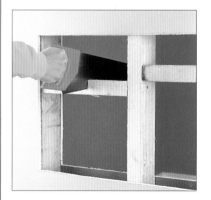

5 Leaving the central stud in place, cut and fit blocks to either side of it at the top and bottom of the opening. It is best to use screws for this purpose, because trying to angle in nails with a hammer can push the blocks below the edge of the opening, making them difficult to pull out of the wall and back into the required position. Make pilot holes for the screws first, as this will help to avoid applying too much pressure on the blocks when fastening them in place.

6 Cut out the central stud, keeping the saw blade flush with the top or bottom of the opening.

7 Trim out the opening with 1 x 6in (2.5 x 15cm) planed softwood. Nail measured lengths in position, beginning with the base followed by the top of the opening and finishing with the two sides. Trim nails are best for this situation. Their heads can be filled before painting the trim.

8 Use the miter saw to cut casing and fit it around the opening on both sides to finish off the project.

Wire nails can again be used for fastening. In addition to nailing the casing through the front, use one smaller nail at each corner of the opening, going through one section of casing and into the adjacent section. Adding a little glue also helps to pull the corner joints together and reduce the risk of any movement, which can potentially cause cracking.

LOAD-BEARING WALLS

These illustrations show how to insert a pass-through in a non-load-bearing stud wall. However, if the opening is to be inserted into a load-bearing wall or a brick or block wall, the technique will need to be modified. In fact, the procedure is similar to removing a load-bearing wall (see page 42). The scale of the project will be reduced as you are dealing with a smaller opening for a pass-through. However, a lintel or header of some sort will be required to fit the opening. Before making the opening, remember to create the proper support for the wall—for a masonry wall, use a needle brace (see page 42) and for a wood-frame wall, build a temporary wall parallel to the existing wall to support the ceiling.

A pass-through provides a useful and attractive access point between two rooms. It can also draw light into dark areas of the home and makes a handy display area.

soundproofing walls ⚡⚡⚡

The best time to soundproof a wall is during its construction, but unless you are physically building a new wall yourself, this option does not often arise. Manufacturers have now come to recognize this rather basic problem and have, accordingly, developed a number of systems to make soundproofing existing walls a feasible and effective procedure, including better insulation slabs, which are now tested to a much higher standard.

By far the greatest need for wall soundproofing tends to arise with walls that you share with a neighbor.

soundproofing a common wall

tools for the job

pry bar
tape measure
pencil
hand saw
cordless drill/driver
torpedo level
protective gloves
dust mask
hacksaw
caulking gun

Traditionally, soundproofing a common wall would usually mean building a new stud wall in front of the existing wall, and using insulation blankets to fill the gap. The dimensions involved would almost certainly mean losing a sizeable area of your own room, as well as requiring some fairly major construction. However, the method below only encroaches 2–3in (5–7.5cm) into the room space, and is therefore rarely noticeable in terms of the overall room dimensions. Proprietary drywall panels are used for this technique—these consist of two different thicknesses of drywall joined together, with another soundproofing layer sandwiched in between. Although this is the ideal material, you can use normal drywall sheets so long

as the bottom layer is of a greater thickness than the top layer. (This adheres to a basic soundproofing theory—when layering similar materials, never use the same depth of material twice.)

1 Score the caulk joint on top of the baseboard before prying it away from the wall with a pry bar. Try not to damage the board as this can be reused later, when the soundproofing is complete.

2 Starting at floor level, use a pencil to make a series of measurements along the corner of the wall, at 2ft (60cm) intervals. It is unlikely that the height of the wall will

fit exactly into divisibles of 2ft (60cm), so simply make the last mark directly at ceiling level.

3 Cut a resilient channel to the exact length of the wall you wish to soundproof, and fasten it in position at floor level. Make sure that the open side of the resilient channel is facing up, and that the fastenings are made just above the floor level. Screw the bottom edge of the channel into the framing.

4 Position a second channel at the next measurement, this time ensuring that the open side of the soundbreaker is facing down to floor level. Use a torpedo level to ensure

that the bar is positioned precisely level. Continue to fasten resilient channel at the marked-off intervals right up to ceiling level. All bars from the second one up should have the open side facing downward.

5 Fit sound insulation beginning at floor level. Lip the bottom edge of the insulation into the open side of the floor level channel, and fit the top edge into the open side of the channel above. So long as your measurements have been made correctly, a precise fit should be achieved. Make sure that you wear protective gloves for this process because the sound insulation fibers can be irritating to the skin, and the channel edges can be sharp.

6 When the bottom section of the wall is complete, progress to the next level, inserting slabs in a similar fashion. Bear in mind that at this and subsequent levels, it is not possible to lip the bottom edge of the slab into the channel. However, the top edge will be lipped into the bar, allowing the

bottom edge of the slab to rest flush on the top edge of the bar below. Continue to fit slabs until the entire wall is covered.

7 Once trimmed and cut to fit, attach the double plasterboard or drywall panels to the wall. Using drywall screws, fasten through the lower level of the panels and into the resilient channel. Screws should be long enough to fasten the board firmly to the channel, but not so long that they reach the original common wall. Otherwise, an automatic channel for sound transfer will be created.

8 Lip the staggered edge of the next panel over the first, butting it up tightly to create a flush joint. It may be easier to put marks along the previous sheet, identifying the exact position of the last fastener. These will indicate the position of the resilient channel and therefore allow you to position the next fastener exactly. Continue to fit panels as required, fastening along the channel at 6–8in (15–20cm) intervals.

9 Finally, apply a bead of caulk around all the new joints made between the plasterboard or drywall panels and the existing floor, walls, and ceiling. The wall may then be plastered or taped and finished, its baseboard reapplied, and painted.

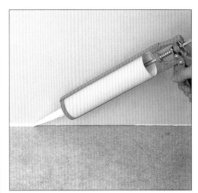

CARPET SOUNDPROOFING

Bear in mind that soundproofing efficiency will benefit from laying good quality padding and carpet in the room. This situation may be further improved by using a specially designed acoustic flooring underlayment system. Even though padding and carpet are more generally concerned with the floor of a room, they will indirectly assist the soundproofing of a wall. This is especially the case if the floor is suspended, which enables noise to travel more easily from one room to another level. So deal with floor soundproofing issues at the same time as dealing with walls.

tips of the trade

Different tools will be required for marking and cutting different materials. Resilient channel should be marked with a felt-tip pen before cutting with a hacksaw or aviation snips. Sound insulation should be marked with chalk and cut with a utility knife. (A dust mask is also vital for this process.) Plasterboard or drywall panels can be marked with a pencil and cut with a utility knife—see page 51.

building a block wall

Although stud walls (see pages 48–51) are easier to construct than solid block walls, there are some instances when a block structure may be more appropriate. For example, in a house where all existing walls are of a block or brick construction, a stud wall may be out of character. Block walls also provide better soundproofing qualities and are better suited to supporting heavy objects or multiple fasteners. Note that they can only be built on footing designed to support the weight of the wall and not on wood framing.

tools for the job

torpedo level

pencil

tape measure

cordless drill/ driver

hammer

gauging trowel

bricklaying trowel

hand sledge

brick chisel

goggles

protective gloves

1 Use a torpedo level and pencil to draw a vertical line on the wall from the floor to the ceiling. This will be the line on to which the wall profile is attached, helping to "tie in" the blocks to the existing wall structure. Profiles vary slightly in design but most will require holes to be drilled for the fasteners. (Use the masonry bit specified by the manufacturers of the profile.) Hold the profile steadily in position on the wall surface and carefully drill through it into the wall surface beneath.

2 Plug the holes and insert the supplied fasteners. Coach screws are often provided for this purpose, and are used in combination with a large washer to add extra strength and rigidity to the fastening. Position them by hand and tighten with a spanner or a plier wrench. Continue to add coach screws up the entire length of the profile. Once the profile is fastened in place, repeat steps 1 and 2 to fasten the second profile to the opposing wall.

3 Attach a string line to the wall to one side of the profile. It should be in such a position that when the first block is positioned, the line will

safety advice

Block walls are quite heavy, so it is important to check that the weight is supported by the floor below. At ground level this is less of a problem, especially on a solid concrete base, but building on a suspended wooden floor is a different matter and you should seek professional advice. Also, when building on second floors or above, similar approval should be sought because joists may need extra strengthening.

correspond to the face of the block and slightly below its top edge. A block may be positioned "dry" to gain the appropriate fastening point. The other end of the line should be attached to the corresponding position next to the other wall profile. This line will help with positioning the first layer.

4 Apply a strip of mortar to the floor, extending away from the profile, and of a width and length slightly wider than a standard block. Try to keep this mortar base a consistent but uncompacted level.

5 Take the first block and mold a cap of mortar on to one end using a gauging trowel. This process

is known as "buttering" and is an integral part of the block- or brick-laying technique.

6 Lift and position the buttered end of the block tight up against the wall profile, while settling the base of the block into the mortar bed. The block weight will force mortar out from underneath it while finding a good, solid resting position.

7 Tap the block with the butt end of the bricklaying trowel to help it settle and check that the front face of the block rests just against the string line, and that it is level.

8 Use a torpedo level to make any final adjustments, ensuring that the block is both level and vertical across the appropriate dimensions as required. After final positioning, continue along the floor, adding blocks, checking levels, and adjusting as necessary until the entire first course of blocks is complete. Trim excess mortar with a trowel as you progress and use it as the base for the next block, together with any extra fresh mortar that is required.

9 Apply a layer of mortar along the top of the first course of blocks to a similar depth as used at ground level. Also, use the ties provided by the profile kit to link into the profile itself and bed into the mortar layer.

10 The most essential rule of block wall construction is to ensure that mortar joints on adjacent levels never coincide. Therefore, before starting the second layer, cut a half block using a hand sledge and brick chisel. Always wear goggles when carrying out this

procedure to protect your eyes from flying debris. Use a sturdy surface to prevent the block from toppling.

11 Add the half block before continuing along with full blocks for the remainder of the course. Keep checking levels at regular intervals and move the string line up to correspond with the next block level. Never lay more than five courses of blocks in one session, and allow them to dry before progressing with additional courses.

openings

It is likely that an opening of some sort will be required in the wall. Simply mark out the dimensions on the floor and build up to these guidelines, leaving the opening block free. Once you have reached the required height for the entrance, a lintel will need to be installed at the top of the opening before you can continue adding blocks, then building up to ceiling level can be completed.

installing wall ventilation ⚒⚒

Effective ventilation is an essential part of any household construction, both for general efficiency and health and safety. Before double glazing and improvements to insulation, installing ventilation systems was never necessary because drafts were a "normal" feature of most houses. However, increased efficiency of insulation in most modern houses means that artificial devices must be installed as substitutes for what was once an automatic system.

AREAS FOR VENTILATION

Key areas for ventilation include:

● **Bathrooms and kitchens**— Bathrooms are an environment in which moist air is pervasive. Adequate ventilation is therefore vital to prevent mold or dry rot, and condensation that can ruin paintwork. Similarly, kitchens can be exposed to steam and condensation, as well as cooking fumes that need good ventilation. Both rooms tend to require mechanical ventilation, such as a bath fan that actually takes air out of the room and to the exterior of the house.

● **Crawl spaces**—Crawl spaces require ventilating beneath them using air bricks in the exterior wall. Failure to install air bricks or allowing them to become blocked can cause problems such as dry rot.

● **Chimney breasts**—When a fireplace has been blocked off, it will be necessary to install a vent in the chimney breast to allow air circulation in the chimney void. The same end can be achieved by installing air bricks on the exterior wall into the chimney void. However, the interior method tends to be easier to carry out and is equally effective.

● **Furnaces and solid fuel fires**— These systems must be vented correctly to ensure that fumes are not allowed to build up inside the house. Always seek professional advice from a qualified engineer and have appliances checked regularly.

installing a through-wall vent

tools for the job

stud finder

tape measure

pencil

hole saw and bit

protective gloves

goggles

dust mask

hacksaw

caulking gun

1 Mark off on the wall the center point for the ventilation shaft. Check for any cables with the stud finder and ensure that the height and position of the hole adheres to any relevant building regulations.

2 Attach the hole saw bit to the main drill body, ensuring that it is correctly fitted in place. Read the guidelines provided by the manufacturer for this process as techniques vary with heavy-duty tools.

3 Position the pilot drill point on the marked wall point and start drilling. The pilot drill will make the initial hole in the wall to secure the hole saw in place and allow the larger round hole saw bit to begin cutting the hole in the wall surface. Be sure to hold the drill firmly as it is both heavy and can "kick" as it bites into the wall surface. Goggles must be worn to protect eyes from flying debris, and a mask is also important as the drill can generate a lot of dust. Ear plugs may also help.

When the drill reaches the other side of the wall, there is a danger that it will blow out the exterior finish or bricks, thus causing a larger hole than required, which will need repair. To prevent this, the drill can be used from both sides of the wall, so that the breakthrough point is inside the wall

safety advice

It is important to get professional advice before installing or changing ventilation systems. This is vital when dealing with the requirements for fuels such as gas, oil, or solid fuels as failure to vent correctly can endanger life.

itself. Advance the pilot bit so that it penetrates through the wall well before the hole saw bit does. When it has pierced the other side of the wall, stop and finish drilling from the opposite side of the wall.

4 Remove the cut core by hand. It should come out in one or two large pieces depending on the wall makeup. If you are drilling through a cavity wall, ensure that no large pieces of the core fall into the cavity.

5 Line the hole with some duct pipe, cutting it to the right size with a hacksaw or tin snips. The

tips of the trade

Installing a passive ventilator in an exterior wall is a straightforward process, as long as you have the correct equipment and tools. It will be necessary to rent a hole saw and bit from your local rental store—such equipment is expensive to buy, and is not worth purchasing for such small jobs such as this.

ductwork can be bought as part of a kit and the manufacturer's guidelines for positioning should be included.

6 Seal around the edge of the ductwork with silicone, ensuring a good unbroken seal. Carry out this process on both the interior and exterior of the wall. (If areas around the edge of the hole broke away or became damaged while drilling, repair them with mortar followed by all-purpose filler, before applying sealant.)

7 Internally, fasten a louver vent to cover the hole. This must be a static ventilator made of metal or

plastic so that it cannot be closed off and inhibit ventilation. Plastic vents may be painted to match and therefore blend with the wall colour, making them a less noticeable feature.

8 On the exterior, fit an exhaust cover over the hole. This enables a good flow of air while limiting strong gusts of wind. It also prevents rain from penetrating through the vent into the room.

9 Again, seal around the exhaust cover with more silicone sealant to ensure a good seal.

tips of the trade

Where electrically operated ventilation fans need to be installed, it will be necessary to seek the help of a qualified electrician in order to ensure that the fan is wired safely to code. An electrician will also provide advice on the positioning and type of ventilation required to provide sufficient air flow and circulation for the room in question.

building a glass-block wall ⚒⚒⚒

Glass blocks provide an unusual alternative to more traditional wall structures, and produce a highly decorative finish that adds character to any room surroundings. They cannot be used for structural support, but they do fulfill the majority of roles required by most walls and make ideal shower walls or room dividers. Extremely versatile, they can even be used to construct curves—thus adding interest to a wall surface and providing attractive, translucent properties.

tools for the job

torpedo level

pencil

nail and line

hammer

cordless drill

gauging trowel

sponge

1 Use a torpedo level and pencil to draw a plumb line on the wall surface, extending from ground level to the finished wall height. As with block walls (see pages 58–9), attach a string line at a height just below the top of where the first course of glass blocks will be, and where it will touch the face of the blocks. You may wish to hold a glass block in place to obtain the correct height and position measurements. Secure the line in the corresponding position on the opposite wall.

2 To add strength to the finished wall, it will be necessary to build a rigid steel framework inside the glass block structure. These steel rods need to be positioned every four to five courses (depending on the manufacturer's guidelines). In order to get the bottom course position for these rods, hold a block "dry" in place at the base of the wall—on top of spacers—to ensure that it is at the correct height. Hold a steel rod on top of the block and mark the position at which it touches the wall surface.

3 Remove the block, spacers, and rod, and drill into the wall surface at the marked-off point. Measure the area required for the block and spacer, and mark off the points at which the rods will be inserted. The marks are made now as drilling later will be difficult.

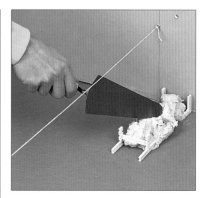

4 Mix up mortar as recommended by the manufacturer. (Use white cement as this has a more pleasing finish with translucent bricks than the other, traditional types of mortar.) Use the spacers to position a block. Then remove the brick and apply mortar to the area between the spacers.

5 Take a glass block and "butter" one side with some mortar, ensuring a good even coverage, trying to keep the mortar off the glass faces of the block.

6 Position the block back on the spacers so that the buttered end is against the wall, with the adjacent edge bedding down into the

mortar on the floor level. Ensure that the block is level and vertical using the spacers—the block should rest against the edge of each spacer.

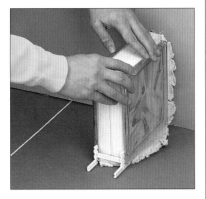

7 Position spacers and add blocks until the entire first course is complete. Use a torpedo level to ensure that the block positions are precise. The top edge of each block should also rest against the string line. Insert a steel rod into the predrilled hole at the top of the first course of blocks.

8 Continue adding courses in the this way until the wall is complete. Remove the face plates of the spacers.

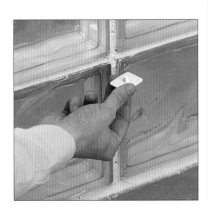

9 Once the blocks have dried out, they can be grouted using a similar mortar mix as used for the building process. Work mortar into any gaps in the joints and smooth to a finish with a clean, damp sponge. The blocks will need wiping several times to remove all mortar residue and leave a clean, bright glass-block surface. If the wall is to be used in a

shower stall, use waterproof tiling grout, and seal the edge of the wall with silicone sealant.

wooden floors

When building on wooden floors, fasten a wooden sole plate to the floor to act as the base for the block wall. Ensure that the wood is the same width as the glass blocks.

spacers

The spacers provided with glass block walls are designed so that they can be adapted to make both T and L shapes, and therefore deal with all requirements in a block wall construction. Simply snap off the parts of the spacer that you do not need.

Glass-block walls make a very distinctive feature, helping to lighten rooms and creating an attractive, decorative effect.

installing a faux fireplace ✂✂

Fireplaces have always had a dual function—in addition to providing heat, they provide a focal point and therefore contribute decoratively to the room as a whole. The advent of central heating meant that many fireplaces were blocked up, but their aesthetic value is now enjoying a revival and these features are reappearing. Solid-fuel and gas fires require professional installation, but building a fireplace for aesthetic or ornamental purposes is relatively straightforward.

fitting a surround

This fireplace was made from pieces of marble and wood from various sources. Marble is a heavy stone, so make sure that your subfloor can handle the weight. (It should be at least 1⅛in (3cm) thick.) You may prefer to get the marble cut to size by a professional. Marble is fragile, so provide plenty of support for it while it is being positioned and while the mortar is drying. The surround is made from stained softwood.

tools for the job

pencil & tape measure

gauging trowel

sponge

torpedo level

pointing trowel

screwdriver

caulk gun

sponge

1 Having chosen your location for the fireplace, mark its central position on the wall surface.

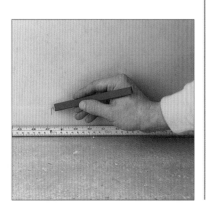

2 Measure from the marked point on the wall surface and draw in the dimensions of the hearth on the floor. Use a trowel to apply a number of mounds of mortar within the confines of the hearth guideline. Make sure the mounds are of a consistent size, so that when the hearth is positioned, it will bed down as evenly as possible.

3 Lift the hearth into place and check that it is centered on the wall mark with a tape measure. Allow the hearth to bed down into the mortar. Check for any mortar squeezing out from under the hearth edges and remove it with a clean, damp sponge before it dries.

4 Use a torpedo level to check the hearth positioning across all dimensions—side to side, front to back, and diagonally—as it will not be possible to make adjustments later.

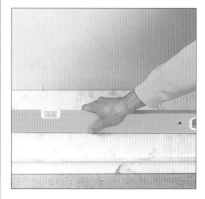

5 Add mounds of mortar to the back panel and position it centrally on the hearth. Allow the panel to secure to the wall, but do not press it finally into position. Check it is sitting plumb by using a torpedo level.

6 Carefully lift the fire surround into position, pushing the back panel onto the wall until the surround is flush against the wall surface. This will also help to force the back panel into its correct position.

7 Remove the fire surround and seal around the edges of the back panel using some more mortar (a pointing trowel is ideal for this process). However, take care not to get any mortar on to the marble face—if this happens, remove it immediately with a clean, damp sponge before it dries.

8 Reposition the fire surround on the back panel. Secure it in place using glass plate fastenings, which will help it to sit flush on the wall surface. Attach the fastenings under the mantel shelf so that they will not be too conspicuous.

9 Finally, attach the internal brass surround to the back panel with some silicone sealant. The surround can be pressed into position by hand. Before it sets, be sure to remove any excess silicone that squeezes out with a dry cloth.

MORTAR CHOICE

Mortar made from white cement is ideal for marble fireplaces because of its aesthetic qualities. Fireplaces may also be positioned using bonding coat plaster, but when using light-colored marble, bear in mind that marble can stain easily. Also, some marble types have transparent characteristics, which will mean that the fixing material may be visible in places. For this reason, a light-colored mortar is best as it should be less noticeable than many of the darker types. Modified white marble mortar has latex added for better performance and is available from home improvement outlets.

Once blended into the rest of the decoration, a faux fireplace can make a stunning impact on the look and feel of a room. Painting the internal "fireplace" matte black creates the impression of an authentic old fire instead of a newly installed reproduction.

altering the structure of a ceiling

When redesigning a room layout or planning a new color scheme, it can be common to neglect ceilings or assume that their finish will be led by other design elements in the room. However, this does not have to be the case, and entering any renovation project should include close consideration of ceiling improvements and potential alterations. Therefore, appropriate heights, soundproofing, access, and insulatory properties are all considered in this chapter, together with ideas for finishing.

Different patterns and designs make suspended ceilings an unusual alternative to traditional ceiling finishes.

lowering a ceiling—1

The most common reasons for lowering a ceiling are to install new duct work or plumbing or to reduce the height of a room for decorative or soundproofing purposes. High ceilings are most common in older properties, but ceiling levels can be adjusted in any room—regardless of age—provided the practicalities of head clearance and final appearance are considered. A two-part process, the first step is to construct a framework for the plasterboard or drywall.

making the frame

Before focusing on the ceiling itself, it is important to consider the existing wall construction. The new ceiling will be supported primarily by fasteners to the walls in the room, and so the strength of these fasteners is vital. For solid block walls, concrete anchors or frame fasteners can be used with confidence because the strength of the fastener will be consistent on all wall areas. If you are fastening to stud walls, however, it will be necessary to locate the studs before you begin. Wall plates can then be fastened directly into the studs, rather than into the surrounding, weaker plasterboard or drywall. Joist hangers, brackets used to support the ends of joists, are recommended for all applications.

tools for the job

tape measure
pencil
level
hand saw
cordless drill/driver
hammer

1 Having decided how far you need to lower the ceiling level, use a pencil and level to mark out a guideline around the entire perimeter walls of the room. Never simply measure the distance at different points and join them together, as slight

ensuring accuracy

Taking extra time to ensure accurate measurements, and that the joists are correctly aligned, will be highly beneficial when it comes to applying plasterboard or drywall to the framework. Even small discrepancies between joist levels will be accentuated once the panels have been applied. It is also vital that the joists are not fastened in the hangers in a twisted position. Otherwise, when panels are applied they will not fit flush against the bottom of the joist, resulting in weak fastenings along the entire joist length.

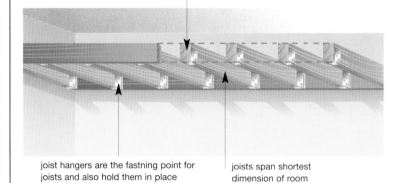

joists set at 2ft (60cm) centers

joist hangers are the fastning point for joists and also hold them in place

joists span shortest dimension of room

variations in most ceiling surfaces mean that these measurements do not provide a true level. It is better to mark off height at one point and use the level from that point on to draw your guideline.

tips of the trade

Modern ceilings are normally 8ft (2.4m) high and manufacturers make most building boards to these dimensions. This is a good guideline to follow when you come to deciding on the height at which to set your ceiling. The joists used for the frame on this page measure 2 x 4in (5 x 10cm), which is the minimum that should be used in such cases. For spans that are greater than 6ft (1.8m), joists should be 2 x 6in (5 x 15cm) or even wider still. Plasterboard and drywall thickness can affect the position of joists. When you are using ½in (12.5mm) drywall, place the joists in position at 16in (40cm) or 24in (60cm) intervals.

2 Cut lengths of 2 x 4in (5 x 10cm) framing to each wall width dimension. Fasten them with the bottom edge of each plate running along the pencil guideline. In this example, the wall plates are being attached with concrete anchors because the walls are solid-block construction. If you are attaching to stud walls, you will need to use a stud finder to find the studs and therefore the ideal positions for fastening.

3 The joists for the frame should always span the room across its shortest dimension, so mark off 2ft (60cm) intervals along the appropriate opposing wall plates, or whatever interval you are using, to denote the position for the metal hangers that will be used to support the joists.

4 At each marked-off point on the two wall plates, partially nail a hanger in place—leave it free enough to adjust when the joist is in place.

5 Cut joists to the exact size between the opposing wall plates, positioning the cut joist inside the hangers. First, use hanger nails to nail the hanger into the sides of the joist to clamp it in place. Then nail the hanger into the wall plate face for a secure, final attachment. Continue to attach joists to hangers across the rest of the ceiling framework.

6 For extra rigidity, add blocking between joists. The blocking should be staggered on either side of the midline of the joists. The ceiling is now ready for plaster-board or drywall.

split level ceilings

Some people choose split-level ceilings as an alternative to a complete ceiling level change. This is ideal for rooms in which high windows prevent the possibility of lowering the entire ceiling, or for people who want variation in the room height. The same basic system can be used to construct the frame, with some slight modifications to the main structure.

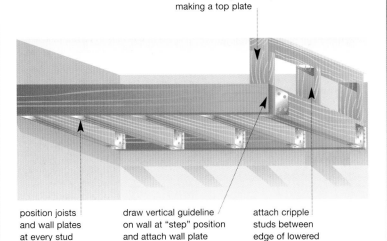

attach framing to ceiling, making a top plate

position joists and wall plates at every stud crossing

draw vertical guideline on wall at "step" position and attach wall plate to existing ceiling

attach cripple studs between edge of lowered ceiling and top plate

lowering a ceiling—2 ✂✂

Once the frame of your lowered ceiling is in place, plasterboard or drywall needs to be fixed in position before plastering or finishing can begin. Large sheets of plasterboard or drywall can be difficult to handle (see below) but lath is an ideal option since it comes in smaller sheets. This is also the point at which additional features such as soundproofing or lighting fixtures should be considered. All of these tasks are quite straightforward, provided you plan ahead.

PLASTERBOARD/DRYWALL

If you are using regular-sized plasterboard or drywall, you will need help lifting and maneuvering the boards. Nail plasterboard at 6in (15cm) intervals along all the joists and drywall at 12in (30cm) intervals. The joints between each sheet should be made half-way across the width of the joists. This will ensure that the edges of two sheets join along a single joist.

plasterboarding with lath

Lath is much smaller and easier to handle than large plasterboard, which makes it much better for maneuvering and enables you to work alone. It is also ideal to use when joists are set on 2ft (60cm) centers because it tends to be supplied in 2 x 4ft (60 x 120cm) sheets, which means it does not require cutting, except for around the perimeter of the ceiling.

tools for the job

hammer

screwdriver (optional)

hand saw

protective gloves

1 Starting in one corner of the room, attach a single lath across three ceiling joists. Plasterboard nails are ideal for this process or, alternately, drywall screws can be used.

2 Continue to add lath to the joists, staggering the joints to create a brick bond pattern. This means that as you reach the perimeter of the ceiling, you will need to measure and cut lath to fill the various gaps.

soundproofing

Lowering a ceiling also provides the perfect opportunity to add some soundproofing to the room. By inserting sound insulation into the ceiling space before plasterboarding or drywalling, you can make a substantial difference in the amount of noise audible from the room above. (An alternative

soundproofing technique is outlined on pages 74 5 where lowering the ceiling level is not an option.)

1 Weave 4ft x 2ft x 4in (120 x 60 x 10cm) sound insulation between the top of the joists and the existing ceiling. If you have not been able to bring the ceiling down this far, use sound insulation of the same size but with a 2in (5cm) depth instead of 4in (10cm). Rest the batts in position, so that they are loosely joined but wedged securely above each joist.

2 Nail plasterboard or drywall sheets to the ceiling (see box). Bear in mind that it is important to use large sheets in this case, rather than

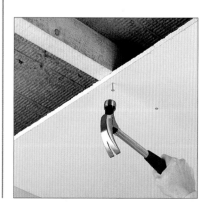

lath, as the fewer the joints, the greater the soundproofing effect. Then apply a second layer of plasterboard or drywall (see step 4 page 74).

fixture canopies

Ceilings tend not to have too many obstacles, and therefore lowering one can be a fairly trouble-free task. The main exception is a fixture canopy, which needs to be adjusted or lengthened in order to be of use for the new ceiling level. This work should be carried out after the new joists have been positioned, but before drywalling has begun.

tools for the job

screwdrivers (various)

cordless drill

hammer

pencil

tape measure

1 Unscrew the canopy by hand, allowing the cover to slide down the wire to the fitting itself.

2 Unscrew the retaining screws that are keeping the canopy secured to the old ceiling. Put the screws safely to one side as they will be needed again later.

3 Release the electrical wires from the canopy by unscrewing the relevant terminals, allowing the wires to drop free. The pendant should now be separate from the electrical cable, and can be put to one side.

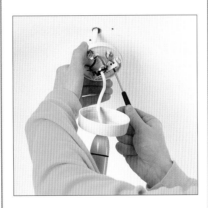

4 Use insulation tape to tape up each wire in the electrical supply cable. Ensure that each wire is completely separated from the others.

5 Drywall the ceiling until you come to a point where the old electrical cable is about to be covered. Drill through the drywall directly below the cable, using a bit that is wide enough to accommodate the cable.

6 Pull the cable through the hole before continuing to apply drywall across the rest of the ceiling. If the cable is too tight in its original position and does not have the required excess to pull down to the new ceiling level, it will be necessary to add extra cable to the existing one, joined with a junction box. Once the ceiling has been plasterboarded or drywalled, the fixture can be reconnected.

building a suspended ceiling ⁊⁊⁊

Suspended ceilings are traditionally associated with offices and commercial buildings. However, such ceiling structures are becoming increasingly popular in private dwellings. They are an ideal option for lowering ceilings, and they require less structural work than alterations using joists and plasterboard or drywall. The tiles provided for suspended ceilings also tend to have both thermal and sound-insulating properties and therefore make a useful alternative to traditional ceilings.

The construction of a suspended ceiling is a straightforward exercise as long as sufficient planning time has been allowed. It is worth drawing a scale diagram of the room in order to work out tile positioning and thus the ideal location for the main tees in the framework (see diagram below).

1 Draw a level pencil line around the perimeter walls at the suspended ceiling height. Fasten wall angle sections along this line at 1ft 4in (40cm) intervals. Attaching to solid block walls should be quite easy but you will need to follow the stud pattern (see page 68) on stud walls.

2 Fasten angle brackets into the existing ceiling at measured intervals above the position where the main tees will be.

tools for the job

tape measure
level
cordless drill/driver
hacksaw
side cutters
pliers
hand saw

3 Cut a section of hanger wire to a manageable length— 6–10ft (2–3m) is suitable—and secure one end to a heavy object such as a workbench. Push the other end of the wire into a cordless drill and tighten the chuck until it is held securely in position. Slowly start the drill, causing the wire gradually to tighten until it is completely rigid. This will ensure that the wire has no slack and will make a rigid support when joined between the bearers and the ceiling.

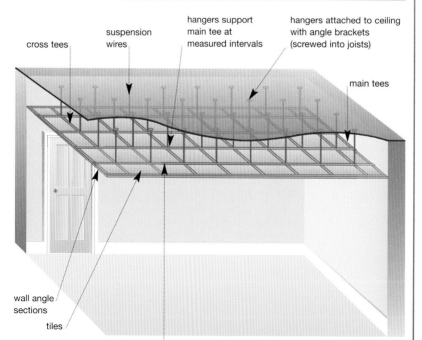

cross tees

suspension wires

hangers support main tee at measured intervals

hangers attached to ceiling with angle brackets (screwed into joists)

main tees

wall angle sections

tiles

main tee framework laid out so that cut tiles are an equal distance from wall around entire perimeter of room

4 Use side cutters to cut the wire down to the required lengths. Allow an excess of 4in (10cm) at each end of the length for attaching to the main tees and angle brackets.

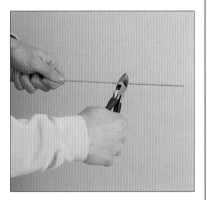

5 At each angle bracket, thread a section of wire through the bracket hole and tighten it in position by wrapping the end of the wire onto the main vertical section with pliers.

6 Position the main tees on the angle sections. Thread the end of the hanger wires through the appropriate holes and wind the ends back onto the vertical length.

7 Fit the smaller cross tees in position, at the appropriate intervals between the main tees. The intervals should correspond to the tile dimensions.

8 Simply drop the tiles in place, feeding them above the suspended ceiling level first and then lowering them into position between the tees. There is no particular insertion order, but it is always best to position the full tiles first before working around the edges. (The edge tiles may be cut using a hand saw or utility knife before they are fitted in place.) Some manufacturers provide clips that fit on top of the tees to hold the tiles down in position.

👍 tips of the trade

Main tees need to be cut so that they can fit precisely between the wall angle sections on opposing walls. Mark off the length requirement on the tee, and cut using a hacksaw.

Different patterns and designs make suspended ceilings an unusual alternative to traditional ceiling finishes.

soundproofing a ceiling ✂✂

If you are unable to combine soundproofing with lowering a ceiling (see page 70) it may be necessary to use other techniques for minimizing sound. One method is to lift the floor above and soundproof from above the ceiling in question. Alternately, it is possible to work from below, taking the existing ceiling down and starting from scratch.

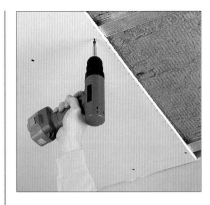

working from below

Soundproofing from below requires the removal of the old plasterboard or drywall. Wearing a mask, gloves, and glasses (see safety note on page 12 for lead and asbestos precautions), break through the first piece and remove sections with a hammer or pry bar.

tools for the job

claw hammer
pry bar
cordless drill
gloves, dust mask, and glasses

1 Carefully remove the old ceiling with a pry bar. Then check between the joists for the presence of wiring or plumbing. Remove any remaining nails with a claw hammer— all joists must be free from obstructions before work begins so that new fasteners can be inserted.

2 Starting on one side of the ceiling, attach resilient channel across the joists at 16 or 24in (40 or 60cm) intervals. Fix the channel in place using drywall screws, ensuring that they are inserted into the joist.

3 Place soundproofing insulation above the resilient channel and between the joists. Try to ensure that the insulation meets and joins above the channel. Continue to position insulation until the whole area is covered. Wear protective gloves for this process as the fibers in the insulation can cause skin irritation.

4 Hang ½in (12mm) plasterboard or drywall sheets to the ceiling using drywall screws. Drive the screws through the sheets and into the resilient channel at intervals. Allow the screws to bite sufficiently to hold the sheets securely in place, but without the screwhead breaking into the surface and creating a weak installation.

5 Attach ⅜in (9mm) plaster-board or drywall sheets over the first layer of sheets, staggering joints so that none of the second layer joints correspond with the first. Longer drywall screws will be required to penetrate both layers and attach into the resilient channel. Tape and set the joints. The ceiling may now be finished or plastered.

tips of the trade

Cove molding is a useful way to introduce an additional soundproofing seal around the edge of the ceiling (see pages 92–3).

working from above

If possible, working from above a ceiling is an easier option for adding sound insulation. Although this involves lifting a floor in order to gain access to the ceiling space, it tends to be less messy than taking a whole ceiling down. Sound insulation is therefore slotted between joists from above, before the floor is relaid. However, where joist depth or the ceiling space is particularly large, sand may be combined with sound insulation to create a more effective soundproofing system.

tools for the job

brick chisel

hand saw

hammer

cordless drill/driver

dust mask

protective gloves

1 Strip the floor back to the subfloor and remove the boards using a brick chisel or small pry bar. Take care not to damage any of the boards as they will be repositioned once soundproofing is complete.

2 Cut sections of 1 x 2in (2.5 x 5cm) batten with a hand saw. Attach the lengths in place along the bottom of the joists, just above the plasterboard or drywall ceiling.

3 Cut and fit ½in (12mm) plywood strips between the joists, attaching them by nailing through the plywood and into the battens.

4 Line the face of the plywood with a plastic membrane sheet. Tuck the membrane into the corners and allow it to encroach up to the top of the floor joists. Nail in position only at the top of the joists.

5 Carefully pour kiln-dried sand onto the plywood between each joist, spreading out the sand into a layer about 2in (5cm) deep. A small piece of batten cut to the width of the

space between the joists makes an ideal tool for spreading the sand across the area and will produce a consistent level.

6 Fit sound insulation in between the joists and on top of the sand. The insulation may need to be cut to fit—use a hand saw or utility knife and wear a dust mask when cutting. Protective gloves should also be worn when fitting the insulation. Then replace the subfloor—a thick padding and good-quality carpet will also add to the soundproofing effect.

safety advice

Remember that sand adds a great deal of weight to the ceiling, so check with a structural engineer that your ceiling will be able to cope with the load. Furthermore, this technique should not be used in ceilings containing water pipes. Any small leaks soaking into the sand over time will increase the weight further and could result in ceiling collapse.

insulating a ceiling ↗

Trying to make your home as energy efficient as possible provides benefits on a financial level and contributes toward protecting the environment. One of the simplest ways to increase energy efficiency is by ensuring that you have adequate attic insulation. This is easy to install but requires some thought about how to deal with any obstacles.

blanket insulation

Blanket insulation is the most commonly used form of attic insulation material as it is the simplest to handle and can be laid very quickly. Roll-length measurements provided by the manufacturer make it easy to estimate the amount required. When measuring, be sure to choose rolls that are the same width (or slightly wider) than the joist bay in your attic. This will help to avoid extra cutting.

tools for the job

protective gloves and dust mask

utility knife

1 Roll out the insulation blanket between the joists. Do not compress it because much of its effectiveness is provided by maintaining its depth. Carefully cut the insulation with a utility knife whenever a division is required.

2 Greater efficiency can be achieved by installing a second layer over, and at right angles to, the first. This technique obscures all the joists, so if you choose this option you may need to build access bridges in your attic.

loose-fill insulation

Loose-fill insulation offers an alternative to blankets. Although it can be used in most situations as a direct alternative, it is mainly used in attics where there are a number of awkward spaces to fill, making it a more practical option than blanket insulation. It is made of similar material to the blankets, but this has been shredded into smaller pieces.

safety advice

Always wear gloves and a dust mask when handling attic insulation as the fibers in its construction can be irritating to both skin and the respiratory system.

tips of the trade

When installing attic insulation, do not cover any ventilation access. Most roof spaces are ventilated through grills or openings in the attic, or at the junction between the roof and exterior walls. Covering these areas can lead to damp and condensation problems, so keep filling safely away from them.

1 Pour the loose fill directly from the bag into the gaps between the joists.

2 Use a piece of batten, cut to the same length as the width of the gap between the joists, to even the loose fill out in the joist gap.

tips of the trade

Just as ventilation inlets must be kept clear of insulation, recessed electrical fittings must also be given clearance, so that they do not overheat. Cut around recessed fittings, leaving plenty of clearance between the insulation material and the fitting.

3 Insulation must always be on top of obstacles rather than below, so make some cardboard bridges for pipes, before covering over them with the loose fill.

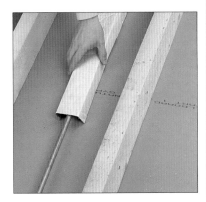

attic access

Attic access panels have to be movable, so it is not possible simply to install insulation on the top of them. However, insulation is still necessary if it is to be effective throughout.

tools for the job

hand saw
hammer
protective gloves
dust mask

1 Cut four pieces of 1 x 6in (2.5 x 15cm) planed softwood to the dimensions of each side of the attic access. Nail them in position to create a shallow box.

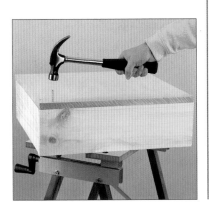

2 Insert a section of blanket insulation inside the box (or loose-fill insulation can be used).

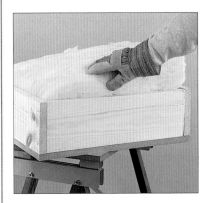

3 Cut a piece of plywood to size, attach it to the top, and position the box as the access panel.

DEALING WITH PIPES

Pipes situated between and below joist level are best dealt with as shown left. However, pipes above the joists need another method of insulation.

Fit pipe insulation over and around any exposed pipes, and butt adjoining sections as required.

Where a junction is required, miter the insulation so that a precise joint is achieved. Insulation can be cut using a utility knife or scissors.

insulating water tanks

The growing popularity of combination boilers means that modern houses are less likely to have attic-situated water tanks. However, some older houses still have water tanks that feed the various systems in the house. It is therefore important to ensure that the tank is insulated correctly.

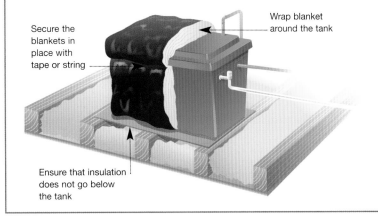

Secure the blankets in place with tape or string

Wrap blanket around the tank

Ensure that insulation does not go below the tank

building an attic access panel ⟩⟩⟩

Many homeowners find the thought of converting their attics into extra rooms or using them for storage in order to free up other rooms an attractive option. Most attics have some sort of access built into the design of the house, but renovation may make it necessary to install a proper access panel.

cutting in an access panel

tools for the job

stud finder
tape measure
pencil
level
drywall saw
hand saw
cordless drill/driver
hammer

Before installing a new access panel, it is important to make all necessary calculations and judgments about its position. If you wish to install a built-in fold-up ladder instead of using a step ladder, ensure that your chosen site has suitable provision for storing it. Also, check to see what is directly above the proposed panel, as precautions must be taken to ensure that services will not be interfered with or disrupted.

The panel must be large enough to allow access for both yourself and any items that need to be passed through the opening. The structure of the ceiling is vital because some joists will have to be cut to make room for the access area. Note that this cutting technique can only be used through conventional framing and not through trusses or engineered materials. It is advisable to seek professional advice before starting, in order to ensure that the ceiling structure will sustain an access panel. In older homes, where joist depth tends to be more

substantial, this is rarely a problem. In newer homes, however, joists tend to be thinner and so it is necessary to check the strength of the structure.

1 Use a stud finder to pinpoint the joist position on the ceiling. Mark out the proposed position of the access panel, ensuring that two of the opposing sides are directly below the edges of two joists. In this way, it will only be necessary to cut through one central joist to create the opening.

2 Wearing a dust mask to protect your nose and mouth (see safety note on page 12), use a drywall saw

to cut around the pencil guideline. On the two sides of the square that run in the same direction as the joists above, try to rest the saw against the joists to achieve an exact cut to the precise joist width.

3 Having removed the plasterboard or drywall, use a hand saw to cut out the central joist. This will provide access through the hole and into the roof space. Trim back the cut joist (from above) another 2in (5cm) at each side of the opening, so that when blocking is inserted to create the opposing sides of the panel, it will be positioned back from the ceiling opening to provide a more rigid structure.

4 Use the hand saw to cut blocking to size, and then screw the blocking in place to form the access panel frame. In addition to attaching the block centrally into the cut joists, it will also be necessary to fasten the corners. Angle screws through the blocking and into the joists at all four corners of the access panel frame with a cordless screwdriver.

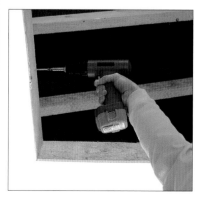

5 Cut 1 x 6in (2.5 x 15cm) planed softwood to the internal dimensions of the opening. Fasten it in place by nailing or screwing directly through the lengths and into the joists and blocking. Ensure the bottom edge sits flush with the ceiling to produce a smooth jamb upon which to attach the remaining features.

6 Cut a ³/₈ x 1in (2.5 x 0.5cm) stop to the internal dimensions of the jamb. Make a pencil guideline around the jamb, halfway up its height. Then nail the stop in place, so that the bottom edge sits precisely on the pencil guideline. This stop will act as the ledge upon which the finished access panel will rest.

7 Measure and cut casing to fit around the jamb. Allow the casing front edge to bisect the edge of the jamb, in order to create a neat and balanced finish.

8 Tighten the mitered joints of the casing by inserting additional nails at each corner, thus pulling the miter together.

9 Cut a sheet of mdf (medium density fiberboard) or finish-grade plywood to the dimensions of the panel and drop it into place above the ledge created by the stop. This can now be primed and painted.

attic ladders

Access through an attic panel can be made by means of a portable ladder or a permanent ladder. Many manufacturers provide easy-to-install ladder systems. If possible, choose your ladder before building an access panel because many manufacturers stipulate dimensions and positioning in order to achieve the best access results. Make sure your ladder is accessible and that the attic has enough clear storage capacity, without obstructing joists.

ensure ladder has room to "fold" in roof space—this will depend on design, so check with manufacturer's guidelines

fit required hinges to attic access

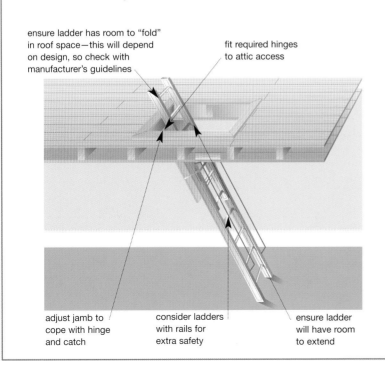

adjust jamb to cope with hinge and catch

consider ladders with rails for extra safety

ensure ladder will have room to extend

constructing a framed ceiling

Framed ceilings offer a purely decorative option to traditional ceiling structure. They can be useful when trying to visually lower a particularly high ceiling, and require less structural consideration than lowering the ceiling in its entirety (see pages 68–71). However, such ceilings require a large quantity of wood and the joinery and measurements used in their construction need to be accurate, in order to achieve the best possible effect.

tools for the job

pencil

level

hand saw

combination square

miter saw

chisel

wooden mallet

cordless drill/driver

1 Draw a level guideline around the perimeter of the room using a pencil and level. This line will be the bottom edge of the framed ceiling, and therefore its positioning should be considered carefully. Height suitability is really determined by the existing ceiling height in your home. Older, more traditional houses vary in ceiling height but modern houses tend to be about 8ft (2.4m).

3 Pencil in a central bisecting line through a small scrap or gauge block of 1 x 4in (2.5 x 10cm) softwood. Hold the gauge block next to each guideline on the full length in turn, marking a second guideline across the length to denote the width of the beams. Then, using the penciled bisecting line on the gauge, mark where this line meets the penciled guidelines on the full length on either side of the gauge.

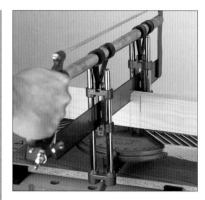

5 Use a chisel to cut out each sawn section of the length. Ensure that the chisel blade dimensions fit exactly between the sawn cuts so as to produce a precise, accurate finish. One light tap with a mallet on the chisel is usually enough to remove this small section of wood. Repeat steps 2–5 for the length of wood required for the opposing wall. It may pay to sand the cutout area lightly to remove any rough edges.

2 Cut a piece of 1 x 4in (2.5 x 10cm) planed, or dressed softwood to the length of the longest wall dimension. Use a combination square to make guidelines at 6in (15cm) intervals along the length.

4 Use a miter saw, set at a 90-degree angle, to cut down to the marks on each guideline on the length. Be exact with this cut, not allowing it to encroach closer than the marked-off points.

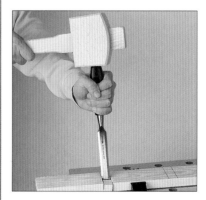

6 Screw the notched lengths into position on the wall, allowing the bottom, uncut edge of the lengths to run along the pencil guideline. Fasten wood screws at every stud crossing—for a masonry wall,

use plugs and screws. On the two opposing walls—as yet untouched—fasten full lengths of 1 x 4in (2.5 x 10cm) dressed softwood between the notched lengths, flush against the wall.

7 Measure exactly between the opposing notches on the two opposing lengths (from wall to wall). Cut lengths of 1 x 4in (2.5 x 10cm) softwood accordingly. At the ends of these lengths, measure in exactly the thickness of the plate—³/₄in (2cm) in this case—and bisect the width of the plate to produce an L-shaped pencil guideline. Cut this portion away, at each end.

8 Position the length between the appropriate notches, allowing the length to drop down into position.

9 A couple of taps with a mallet may be required finally to position the length—fasteners should not be necessary. Repeat this process across the entire ceiling.

tips of the trade

For ceilings where the beam length is more than 9ft 9in (3m) you may need to add extra support. Attach a length of 2 x 2in (5 x 5cm) dressed softwood across the top of the beams, and attach it to the ceiling with straps.

tips of the trade

Dropping the ceiling level will mean that ceiling-fitted lighting will also need adjusting. This may require the lengthening of pendants or fluorescent fittings. Alternatively, a switch to wall-mounted fittings could be an option. Consult an electrician before embarking on this work.

Painting the original ceiling above the beams can enhance the desired effect. The beams themselves can also be used as a system from which to hang decoration.

paneling & lining

Once the basic structure of a room has been altered, additional work is required to get the room ready for finishing touches and decorative features. In particular, it's important to achieve wall and ceiling finishes that are suitable for accepting decorative coatings. This chapter therefore explains the correct procedures for plastering and finishing—both of which are essential skills in the construction finishing process. The remainder of the chapter looks at many other options of a more style-based nature, such as techniques for adding greater interest to wall or ceiling surfaces, in order to personalize the room and produce individual features and characteristics.

Decorative wall paneling makes an attractive finish in any room, especially when used on stairwells.

finishing drywall ⁄⁄⁄

While previously it was explained how to create partitions and attach plasterboard or drywall to wall surfaces, it is also important to achieve some kind of smooth wall finish before decorative layers can be applied. The two most common types of wall finishes are plaster and drywall finish. Drywall finish is, in simple terms, a way of making a smooth joint between drywall sheets. It provides a neat, professional finish to the walls.

drywall finish

Although the basic structure of all drywall is the same, there are slight design variations to help ensure a smooth finish. For finishing, the drywall used for the wall surface should have tapered edges. These edges work in conjunction with joint tape and joint compound, enabling you to achieve a clean, smooth surface.

tools for the job

nail set and hammer
screwdriver
scissors or utility knife
6in (15cm) drywall knife or scraper
sponge
8–12in (20–30cm) drywall knife
sandpaper and dust mask
dusting brush
aviation snips

1 Before starting, check that all nail heads or screws are below surface level. Nail heads sitting slightly

above the surface may be knocked in using a nail set and hammer. However, make sure you punch the nails just below the surface—if they are inserted too far, the drywall may crumble and cause a weak attachment. Drywall screws protruding above the surface can be tightened with a screwdriver.

2 Apply self-adhesive joint tape along the entire drywall joint, smoothing it into place and ensuring that there are no wrinkles or bumps in the tape surface. Cut the tape using scissors or a utility knife.

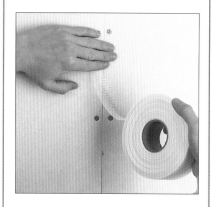

3 Use a drywall knife (or scraper) to press the joint compound into the length of the taped joint. Work

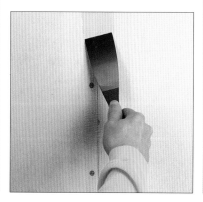

along the joint, making sure that the compound covers the tape. Ensure that the whole joint is coated from ceiling to floor, reworking areas of the joint with more compound if you find it necessary. Allow this to dry.

4 Immediately after applying the compound, smooth any lumpy areas with a clean, damp sponge. Keep rinsing the sponge but be sure to wring it thoroughly, so that it doesn't become soaked. This is because excessive moisture can weaken the joint and cause cracking.

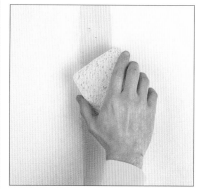

5 Use an 8–12in (20–30cm) drywall knife to apply a wide band of compound down the filled

joint. The knife should span or ride over the tapered sides.

6 After completing all the joints in this fashion, use a drywall knife to add some extra compound over the nails or screw heads. Allow to dry, then repeat the process once more.

7 Once the compound has dried, sand the joints and filled nail heads with fine-grit sandpaper. Use sandpaper wrapped around a block. If you prefer to use an electric sander, be sure to wear a safety mask as it can create dangerous dust.

📖
traditional tip

The technique described here uses self-adhesive joint tape, which is a relatively new development. A more traditional method uses a joint tape that is not self-adhesive. In this case, the compound is added to the joint and then the tape applied over it. Once the tape is in place, continue as before.

dealing with corners

Corners require a slightly different technique for application, but the principle of taping and finishing sheets of drywall remains the same. Although the self-adhesive joint tape used for flat wall surfaces can be used, it is easier to use special precreased paper tape.

inside corners

1 Use a dusting brush to remove any loose debris or material along the corner. Then apply joint compound along and to either side of the corner junction. Ensure a good, even coverage.

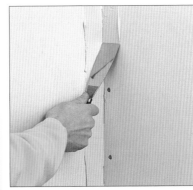

2 Apply corner tape along the junction, pressing it firmly into the joint compound. Ensure that there are no ripples or bumps in the tape surface, and that the central crease of the tape runs directly along the corner junction apex. Cut the tape to fit with aviation snips. (Scissors are insufficient because some tapes contain wire strips.)

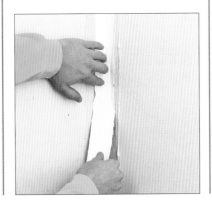

3 Remove excess compound from the corner with a 3in (7.5cm) drywall knife. This helps to secure the edges of the tape. Allow to dry before applying a second layer of compound to cover the tape. Once dry, sand to a smooth finish in the usual way.

outside corners

Corner bead or corner joint tape, which is reversible, are generally used along outside corners. Alternately, an external corner trowel may be used for finishing purposes.

tips of the trade

• In order to achieve the best possible finish, make sure that tools are kept clean. This is especially important with drywall knives, which should be wiped down with a damp sponge after every few applications of compound.

• Remaining compound can be used as an excellent all-purpose filler. However, be sure that it is stored in an airtight container.

• Always allow compound to dry at natural room temperature—excessive heat will cause cracking.

• Fine-grit sandpaper can quickly become clogged when finishing walls. To reduce waste, use old medium-grit paper that has been worn down on other tasks or use drywall sandpaper.

• Once sanded, seal the entire wall surface with a drywall primer before applying paint.

plastering a wall ⁄⁄⁄⁄

Plastering is the traditional method for finishing walls. It is a highly skilled job but, with time and practice, it is possible to produce a good finish. Plaster can be applied directly over plasterboard, or it may be used to finish solid wall surfaces, but only after the appropriate base or scratch preparation coats have been applied.

solid walls

tools for the job

mortar mixing equipment

paintbrush for bonding agent

plastering trowel

gauging trowel

bucket

hawk

Whether block, brick, or natural stone, such solid wall surfaces require a base coat before the plaster can be applied.

MORTAR MIXING

The secret behind achieving a successful base coat is to have the correct mortar mix and consistency. The standard mix is composed of 5 parts builder's sand to 1 part cement, with hydrated lime and waterproofer added according to the manufacturer's guidelines.

Add sufficient water to get the mix into a stiff but smooth consistency, which will allow the mortar to spread across the wall surface easily, but without sagging and therefore losing its shape. Different walls have different absorption properties, so bear this in mind when mixing. Also, uneven surfaces may require a two-coat system, in which case the first should be a stiffer mix of 4 parts sand to 1 part cement.

1 Before application, apply a coat of bonding agent (follow the manufactuer's recommendations) and allow it to dry. Use a plastering trowel to apply the base coat to the wall surface with large, sweeping strokes. Press and smooth as you work, ensuring total coverage. Try not to worry about mortar that squeezes out and falls away on either side of the plastering trowel—the job is a messy one and this sort of excess is to be expected.

2 Smooth over the surface with a plastering trowel to create a flat finish. Then score the surface with the edge of a gauging trowel.

applying plaster

When a solid wall has had a base coat applied and then dried for 48 hours, the technique for applying plaster is very similar to that for applying plaster to plasterboard. The only difference is that plasterboard will need some preparatory work around the joints between different sheets. With a base coat, the wall simply needs to be wetted with bonding agent before applying plaster.

tools for the job

power drill & mixing attachment

bucket

plastering trowel

paintbrush

scraper

1 Tape along all the joints between the plasterboard sheets using self-adhesive joint tape. Press firmly in place, ensuring there are no wrinkles in the tape.

2 Mix multifinish plaster into a smooth, creamy consistency by gradually adding water. If possible, use a power drill with a mixing attachment to stir the mix, since this will help to ensure a thorough blend. If you do use a drill, engage the trigger only when the mixing attachment is safely inside the bucket and plaster—starting the drill outside the bucket can be extremely dangerous.

3 Apply the plaster across the wall surface using a plastering trowel. Make sure that you spread the plaster evenly, pressing down as you move the trowel across the entire wall surface.

4 When the entire wall is covered, smooth the plaster with the trowel to create a completely flat finish. Allow the plaster to dry to a firm but still wet-to-the-touch finish, and "polish" the surface with a dampened plastering trowel. This process takes semidry plaster from the peaks on the wall surface and fills in the troughs, creating a smooth finish across the entire surface.

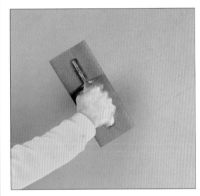

dealing with awkward areas

Every wall surface will normally have some sort of obstacle that hinders the free movement of the plastering trowel. Electrical outlets, which sometimes cannot be removed, are examples of problem areas, but this technique also applies to door and window frames.

1 In the tightest area, such as between the edge of the electrical outlet and the wall or door casing, carefully smooth the plaster with a dampened paintbrush.

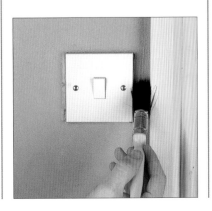

2 Use a dampened scraper on the other corners and sides of the outlet to produce a flat finish.

corners

Corners are commonly encountered when plastering, but generally create little problem, as long as the correct procedure is followed. Professionals tend not to plaster adjacent walls on the same day or, at the very least, they wait until one wall has set before starting the next. In this way, the plastering trowel can be used to scrape down tightly against corner joints, creating a well-defined edge. Alternately, specialized corner plastering trowels may be used to achieve a finish in these areas.

BONDING COAT ALTERNATIVE

One alternative to scratch coat is to apply a bonding plaster coat directly on to block walls. This plaster is very different from finishing-coat plaster, as it has a much coarser and more grainy consistency. Apply it using the same technique as for base coat, although follow the manufacturer's guidelines to ensure the correct mix.

paneling walls—1 ⚒

Wall paneling may either be applied directly over unfinished walls or onto a plastered or drywalled wall. The finish, which is normally wood-based, is designed to provide an attractive feature, although it can also help to prevent wall damage from chairs and furniture. Paneling generally requires a framework base made from lightweight furring.

making a framework

tools for the job

utility knife
pry bar
pencil and level
tape measure
hand saw
power drill
cordless drill/driver
hammer

For entire wall covering purposes, furring should be fixed at the ceiling/wall junction and ceiling/floor junction, with additional lengths in between. For midheight paneling, the top furring strips should be positioned at the height to which you require the paneling to extend. One more furring strip should be positioned equidistant from the top and bottom battens.

1 Score along the top of the baseboard with a utility knife, then carefully pry it from the wall.

2 Use a pencil and level to mark a series of horizontal lines up the wall surface. Start at floor level, marking off every 24in (60cm) until you reach the required height.

3 Cut and fasten furring strips along the guidelines. If the wall is masonry (such as this one) you will need to use a power drill to make pilot holes through the furring and into the wall, ready for screw attachment.

4 Drill a hole and insert concrete anchor screws into the wall surface. For a wood-framed wall, attach screws at every stud crossing.

5 Hold a straightedge (a piece of furring is ideal) across the face of the positioned furring strips. This will help you to check how straight they are on the wall and to see whether the paneling will sit flat when attached. Wavy walls should be shimmed out with wooden shims placed with a hammer. The first wedge may need balancing with a second wedge to keep the face of the furring strip flat and level with the wall surface. Once complete, recheck the straightness of the wall, and proceed with the paneling of your choice.

applying tongue-and-groove paneling

Tongue and groove is an effective way to produce a paneled wall finish. It may be applied from floor to ceiling, but it has greatest effect if it is used up to chair-height level, as shown here. The thickness of the material varies—for this purpose, relatively thin lengths are ideal as they have no structural role and need only to be decorative.

tools for the job

tape measure

hand saw

hammer

nail set

level

1 Cut lengths of tongue and groove to fit between the floor and top edge of the highest horizontal furring strip. Slide the groove of each new length over the tongue of the previous, making a secure joint.

2 Fasten the lengths in place by nailing finish nails through the junction (called the shoulder) made by the tongue and main body of the length, and into the furring strip below. Angle the nail towards the body of the board as shown.

3 Set the nail in farther using a nail set. Continue in this way, so that as subsequent lengths of tongue are added, the nailing of the

previous length is concealed. This blind nailing ensures that there are no visible nail holes.

4 Cut and fasten a length of chair rail to the front top edge of the paneling. A small length of furring may be required along the top edge of the paneling to ensure a smooth finish. Finally, replace the old baseboard or install a new one (see page 96).

tips of the trade

Most walls have obstructions such as electrical outlets and switches. In such cases it will be necessary to cut small openings in the paneling to ensure that these points may be brought forward and securely repositioned. Measure these junctions carefully, and cut out the paneling before fixing it into position.

Whether painted or stained, tongue and groove provides an attractive and durable finish. It helps to break up an expanse of wall surface and adds interest to the look of the entire room.

paneling walls—2 ⚒⚒⚒

Wall paneling can be used to cover entire surfaces, although it is more common to use it in the lower third of a wall. This helps to divide the wall space into two separate areas with different textures and appearance. There are many options and choices of finish that can be used to produce this effect, although traditional looks still have the most popular appeal.

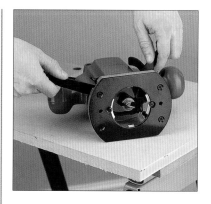

site-made paneling

It is possible to make your own paneling effect using sheets of MDF (medium-density fiberboard). Sheets that are ½in (12mm) thick are ideal as they produce a rigid structure and have good depth. The amount of board required will obviously depend on specific room measurements. When estimating quantities, however, always allow 10–15 percent extra to account for waste. The wainscot here is based on a height of 3ft (1m) from the floor. This is a popular height but you can make paneling fit any dimensions you require.

tools

tape measure & pencil
hand saw
router
dust mask
cordless drill/driver and/or power drill
level
wood glue
hammer

1 Calculate the required size of the squares by measuring the width and height of the area to be paneled. (For an average wainscot height of 3ft (1m), the panels should be around 9–10in [22.5–25cm] each.) Use a tape measure and pencil to mark the required lengths along the edges of the MDF board.

2 Use a length of batten to join up the pencil marks on opposite edges of the MDF, making a grid of equal-size panels. Use a hand saw or circular saw to cut along all the lines, thereby dividing the MDF sheet into a number of equally sized panels.

3 Secure an edge guide to the router. The technique for this procedure will vary with the model,

---

✋ safety advice

When sawing or using a router with MDF, wear a dust mask and protect the work area from spreading dust.

---

so read the manufacturer's guidelines carefully, and adhere to the relevant safety procedures.

4 Clamp a panel to your workbench and run the router along the sides of one of the squares to produce molded edges. Repeat for the other squares. Always work away from your body, and keep a firm grip on the router handles to ensure you have control of the movement.

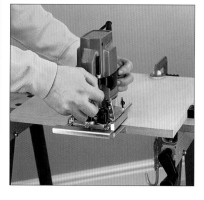

5 Attach furring strips to the wall using the procedure shown on page 88. Measure and cut sheets of MDF to this framework,

to provide a base for the paneling. The sheets of MDF may be fastened in position with wire nails or countersunk screws.

6 Measure off the panel positions along the MDF sheets. For a standard wainscot height of 3ft (1m) allow for two rows of panels, positioned 3in (7.5cm) apart.

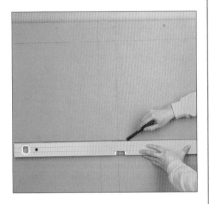

LARGE-SCALE OPTIONS

Paneling choices and options have increased in recent years due to the innovation of manufacturers. Specific laminated finishes are available, as well as more traditional looks, the latter being demonstrated by the examples here.

- **Tongue-and-groove MDF**—It is now possible to buy full-size sheets of MDF pre-routed to provide a tongue-and-groove finish. Enabling large areas to be paneled quickly, the time-saving possibilities are clearly apparent.

- **Pressed paneling**—Site-made panel-effect sheets may be bought and fixed to furring. However, this can be expensive and waste is unavoidable in complicated areas.

7 Apply some wood glue to the back of a routed panel. Be sparing with the adhesive to avoid having excess amounts squeeze out around the edges. Position the panel on the MDF base, carefully aligning it with the pencil marks.

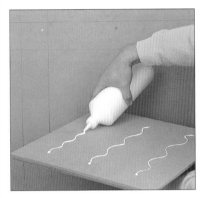

8 Insert three or four nails to add strength to the attachment. Repeat this process for the other panels along the MDF base. Finally, add a chair rail (see page 87), and some baseboard (see page 96), before painting the paneling.

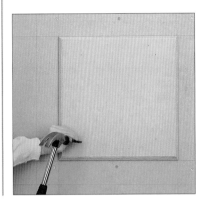

Once prepared and decorated, site-made paneling produces an extremely effective decorative wall finish. Pale colors provide a soothing effect between surfaces and make the most of the depth and texture produced by this finish.

installing cove ✓✓

Cove, sometimes known as cornice, forms a decorative joint between walls and ceilings. Traditional types are made from fibrous plaster but most modern, simple designs are made from gypsum plaster or polystyrene. Polystyrene moldings are cheaper, lighter, and faster to install, but plaster-based cove tends to produce a more attractive finish.

92

fitting plaster cove

tools for the job

pencil
tape measure
level
hand saw
miter box
gauging trowel or scraper
hammer
nail set
sponge
sandpaper

1 Make a pencil guideline around the perimeter of the room. The distance of the guideline from the ceiling should be equal to the exact depth of the cove you have chosen to use. However, this line can only serve as a positional guide because unevenness in the ceiling may throw the edge of the cove off slightly. A corresponding pencil guideline can also be marked on the ceiling if you wish.

2 Measure the distance along each wall at ceiling level. Calculate the lengths of cove required and use a miter box and hand saw to cut the pieces accurately. In the pictures below, inside corners are being shown. Remember to use the opposite angle on the block for outside corners.

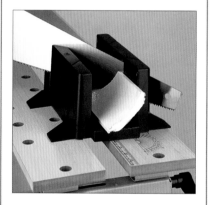

3 Carefully apply cove adhesive along the back edges of the cove length. Use a scraper or gauging trowel to spread the adhesive along the entire edge. However, do not apply adhesive to the central area as it does not come into contact with the wall or ceiling surface.

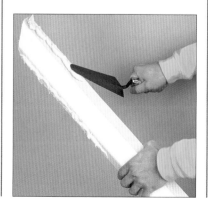

4 Press the length into place using the guideline for positioning. Allow excess adhesive to squeeze out of the joints onto the ceiling and wall, ensuring a good contact along the entire length of the cove.

5 Nail supports to hold the cove in position while the adhesive dries. These may be inserted below the bottom edge of the cove, and removed once the adhesive has hardened. However, it is possible to nail through the cove into the wall, thus making the supports permanent.

6 Wipe away excess adhesive with a damp sponge before it has a chance to dry. At the same time, fill any small gaps along the ceiling and wall junctions with adhesive. Then carefully set the heads of any supporting nails, so that the head sits just below the surface level of the cove. However, do not punch them in too far as this could cause the cove to crack.

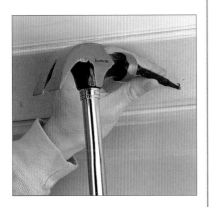

7 Fill the nail heads with some adhesive. Once this dries, a second application may be required to provide a good finish.

8 Continue to add lengths of cove around the rest of the room. Before applying adhesive to each length, check that the miters join correctly by addressing the end of each new length to the previous one, and trimming any small adjustments as required. Once the room has been completely coved and the adhesive has dried, use some fine-grit sandpaper to sand the filled nail holes and cove.

👍

tips of the trade

Instead of using coving adhesive, textured ceiling coatings can be used as the adhesive. This is especially useful if you are combining textured ceiling coatings with coving, as there is no need to buy separate adhesive for fixing purposes.

corner sections

Some manufacturers provide ready-made corner pieces for both polystyrene and plaster cove, therefore eliminating the need for mitering joints. However, despite this easing of the process, a joint is still required between straight lengths and the corner pieces themselves. Therefore, some filling and sanding will still be necessary in order to make these joints as invisible to the naked eye as possible. So, unless the corners are completely square, a better finish is normally achieved by using a saw and miter box. Adjust the angles of the final cuts as required and keep checking your work, since you will want to minimize large gaps and areas for filling.

Cove makes a decorative feature in any room, and it helps to conceal the sometimes awkward junction between the wall and ceiling. Bright white finishes are most popular but any color paint could be applied for an attractive finish.

adding plaster features ⟩⟩⟩

In addition to cove, there are many other accessories that can be used as decorative elements on both ceilings and walls. It is possible to purchase plastic or polystyrene features, but by far the most effective finishes are achieved with fibrous plaster-based materials and gypsum-reinforced plaster. However, bear in mind that such pieces can be heavy and need good support.

paneling

Plaster paneling can be applied to ceilings as well as walls, although ceiling application requires a considerable amount of planning to ensure that the designs are positioned correctly across the ceiling surface. Wall application still requires accurate measuring, but installation is easier.

tools for the job

tape measure
level
sponge
hammer
putty knife

1 Mark out a level line on the wall surface. Apply adhesive to the first length of paneling and position it precisely on the line. Remove any excess adhesive with a damp sponge before it dries.

2 Nail supports below the length to hold it in position while the adhesive dries. The paneling used here is very thin so it is not possible to screw permanent mechanical supports through each panel because this would cause damage or cracking. Therefore temporary nail supports are best.

3 Take the bottom two corner pieces and position them using the pencil guideline. Butt the joints in the same way as for the first panel. Once again, nail temporary supports while the adhesive dries.

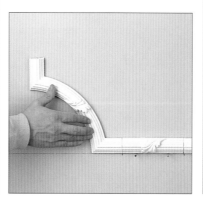

4 Position vertical sides of the paneling using a level. Finish by fastening the final two corners and top length in place, supporting as necessary. Once the adhesive has fully dried, remove the nails, fill the holes, and sand the surface. Continue applying the panels to the wall as required.

building a niche

Substantial and impressive, a niche can be flush-mounted or built into the wall surface. The process for a non-load-bearing stud wall is fairly straightforward, but seek professional advice before working on solid-block and load-bearing walls.

tools for the job

stud finder
drywall saw
hand saw
cordless drill/driver
damp sponge
sandpaper

1 Use a stud finder to locate a suitable area for the niche (there should be adequate support but as few studs as possible). Stick the manufacturer's template to the wall and use it to mark out a pencil guideline. Wearing a dust mask, follow the pencil guidelines and cut out the niche profile with a drywall saw.

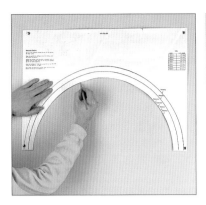

any vertical studs in the way of the niche. Insert a sill plate or block along the bottom of the opening and a header at the top. Insert screws through the sill into the vertical studs at each corner.

position so that its base rests on the sill plate. Remove excess adhesive with a clean sponge.

4 Finally, apply adhesive to the niche plinth and position it below the main niche body. It may be necessary to support the niche as it dries.

2 Remove the section of plasterboard or drywall from inside the niche profile and cut out

3 Apply adhesive around the edge of the niche and push it into

CEILING ROSES

Roses can be used individually or in combination to produce a pattern on the ceiling surface. The rose must have some kind of mechanical support —it cannot rely on adhesive alone.

Once the joist position has been marked, apply adhesive to the back of the rose and hold it in position. Pilot drill and screw fasteners through the rose and into the joists above. Take care not to overtighten since the plaster may crack. When the rose is in place and the adhesive dry, fill the screw head holes and sand before painting.

Once it has completely dried and been painted, a niche provides a superb decorative feature. Adding a light source will enhance the niche's effect on the room decor as a whole, forming an ideal display area for accessories or flowers.

installing baseboards ⁊⁊⁊

Baseboard is the most effective material for finishing the junction between walls and floors. It helps to protect the bottom of the wall from scuffs and dents, but it also provides a decorative feature. This means that, like cove, there is a wide range of designs available and profiles can be chosen to match similar designs for casing around doors, chair rails, and even picture rails. Once the design has been chosen, it's important to spend time installing it properly.

MITER CUTTING

If the baseboard is to butt up against a straight edge such as plinth block or casing, a simple, straight saw cut at the correct measurement along the length is all that is required (see right). However, when lengths need to join at a corner it is necessary to make a more complicated cut.

• **Mitered cuts**—Either a miter box and back saw or a specially designed miter saw can be used for cutting 45-degree angles in baseboard lengths. The miter saw locks in place to allow a precise cut to be made at the correct angle through the baseboard length. The direction of the cut will also be dependent on whether a miter for an inside or outside corner is required.

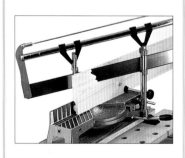

👍 tips of the trade

Most manufacturers now produce baseboard with different profiles on each side. This saves wood but can make measuring and cutting confusing. For this reason, keep checking your board as you measure, cut, and install, to ensure that the correct profile is always being used.

coping

This method should be used exclusively on inside corners. In a simple square corner, allow the end of the first length of baseboard to butt straight up against the wall surface. The second length must now be cut to fit against and around the profile that the first length creates in the corner junction.

tools for the job

tape measure
pencil
back saw
jigsaw or coping saw
plane (optional)
hammer
cordless drill/driver
miter saw

1 Measure the length of baseboard that you require. Then take a cut-off section of baseboard, position it over the length, and draw around its outline with a pencil.

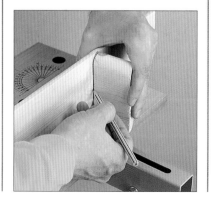

2 Cut the baseboard along the pencil guideline using a jigsaw or coping saw, which makes it easy to follow the curve of the guideline, producing an accurate cut.

uneven floors

In some instances, an uneven floor can make installing baseboard more difficult. This is because the bottom edge of the board is machined to a straight edge and any dips or bumps in the floor will either show as gaps or push the baseboard up. This means that the board will be out of alignment when it comes to meeting the next length in a corner. In such circumstances, it is necessary to scribe the bottom edge of the baseboard so that it will sit flush against the floor surface.

1 Cut the board to the correct length and temporarily position it at the base of the wall. Take a scrap of wood whose thickness is the same as the largest gap between the bottom edge of the baseboard and the floor. Holding a pencil on top of

the scrap of wood, start in one corner, and drag the block and pencil across the floor, next to the baseboard, allowing the pencil to draw a guideline on the baseboard's surface. This guideline reveals the line to cut along, so that when the board is attached, it will follow the profile of the floor without leaving any gaps.

2 Remove the baseboard and clamp it to a workbench. If a substantial amount of wood needs to be removed, cut along the guideline using a jigsaw. If it is only a small amount, shave off the unwanted material with a block plane.

Once cut to fit, the baseboard needs to be attached securely in position. The type of attachment will depend on the wall structure. For stud walls, it is best to nail through the wall into the bottom plate and vertical studs. With masonry, the attachments can be anywhere, as long as they are secure.

nail attachments

Finish nails are ideal for nailing into studwork as their heads are easily concealed and they tend not to split wood. If hammering into block or brickwork, masonry nails should be used. The number and frequency of nails required will be dependent on the strength of each attachment— nails every 16 or 24in (40 or 60cm) will usually suffice.

screw attachments

Screws are often better for attaching baseboard to masonry walls. This is because there can be a tendency for nails to bounce the baseboard away from the wall as subsequent nails are inserted. In other words, you may gain a good attachment with one nail, but the vibration caused by inserting the next nail can weaken the attachment of the first, thus pulling it away from the wall. So use screws, first drilling pilot holes and fastening in place with concrete anchor screws or plugs and screws.

difficult joints

In addition to normal inside corners, there are other areas of the wall where baseboard requires a different approach to attachment, to ensure that the baseboard is secure.

outside corners

Miter joints at outside corners using a miter saw. Once nailed in position on the wall, insert finish nails through the face of one piece of baseboard and through the miter joint with the second length. Applying wood glue to the joint is also a good idea.

lap joints

Rather than butt-joining lengths on open walls, it is always best to make a mitered joint because butt joints tend to crack quickly after painting, leaving an unsightly gap. Instead, miter the joint and apply some wood glue before nailing the joint with two finish nails through the miter.

installing decorative rails ⚒

Decorative rails offer another way of adding character to walls. The rail shape tends to be determined by its function—a picture rail usually has an upturned top edge to provide a stable base for the hook, while chair rails are traditionally used to prevent chairs from damaging the wall surface and so have a rounded surface. Generally, chair rails are fitted about 3ft (1m) from floor level and picture rails are positioned between 8in (20cm) and 20in (50cm) from the ceiling.

paneling & lining

installing a chair rail

Chair rails tend to be the most popular choice of molding, as many modern houses do not have the height to accommodate picture rails. Chair rails can be applied in rooms with low or high ceilings and will produce an excellent effect.

tools for the job

tape measure
pencil
level
miter saw
hammer or cordless drill/driver
nail set
caulking gun
sponge

1 Draw a horizontal guideline around the wall perimeter using a pencil and level. Measure the wall dimensions and calculate the required lengths for each wall. Be sure to get the end of the tape measure right into the corners of the wall.

2 Clamp the molding into the miter saw (to ensure a precise cut) and cut the required lengths.

3 Apply bonding adhesive to the back of the molding. Allow the adhesive to run down the central portion, so that when it comes into contact with the wall it will spread from the center toward the edges.

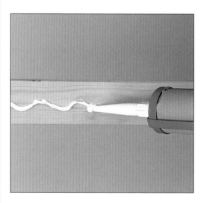

4 Press the molding in position, allowing the pencil guideline to run along either its top or bottom edge. Continue to press in position along the molding's length, so that total contact between the molding and wall is achieved. Use a sponge to remove any excess adhesive.

5 Nail or screw fasteners along the length of the molding to hold it firmly in position, and set the nail heads in below the molding's surface level. Continue to install lengths around the rest of the room.

👍 tips of the trade

When a chair or picture rail is to remain unpainted, avoid using permanent nail fixings, which will be easily visible. Instead, just apply a strong contact adhesive that will hold the molding permanently in position while it dries. Some extra support may be given during the drying process by taping over the molding—the tape will help to bear the molding's weight.

6 Apply a bead of caulk along the top edge of the chair rail, smoothing it into the joint with a wet finger. This will help to cover any small cracks and produce a better surface finish for decorating.

7 Also apply caulk to corner joints, especially where miter joints are not totally tight. Nail heads may then be filled with an all-purpose filler and carefully sanded to a smooth finish before staining or painting.

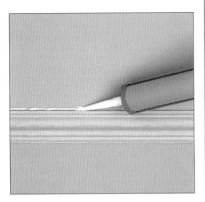

tips of the trade

All dissimilar materials, for example the wood and drywall along the edges of the rail/wall junction, will need to be caulked even if the joint seems masked by strong colors. Caulk will cover the joint and provide a neat finish.

DECORATION

• **Wallpapering**—If the decorative rail is to be used to divide two types of wallpaper, or there is to be a particularly strong contrast between the rail color and the wall, it may be better to paint or stain the rail before it is fastened in position.

Apply wallpaper to the surface before attaching the rail. Even if the rail is to divide two different papers, it is possible to use only rough joints, as the rail will cover this area.

• **Staining**—For a natural or a stained wood finish, apply two coats to the rail before cutting and attaching it, so that there is no need to encounter an exacting staining process along the edge of the rail. This early staining means that you should not have to cut in too closely to the paper when applying a final top coat. This method may also be used with paint.

• **Painting**—If you plan to paint the rail in a strong color, mask off both sides of the wall surface with painter's tape.

Remember that applying rails after painting the wall does make repairing any scrapes or wall damage more difficult, so take extra care when installing the rail.

Decorative rails provide an attractive feature that breaks up wall space while adding character to a room design.

applying embossed wall coverings ⚋⚋⚋

Embossed wall paneling offers a lightweight alternative to wood paneling such as tongue and groove. The application procedure is more similar to that of wallpaper than wood paneling, although the panels are supplied in specific sizes and are generally designed to cover only the chair-rail level in a room.

planning

The predetermined size and patterning of this type of paneling means that you will need to plan its positioning carefully. The aim should be to keep seams in discrete areas, so try to join full panels in corners that are seen every day, and seam half panels in corners that are less obvious.

tools for the job

level

pencil

tape measure

pasting brush and table

sponge

paperhanging brush

straight-blade holder or utility knife

hammer

1 Decide on the best starting position and draw a vertical guideline on the wall with a level.

2 The back of the panels must be soaked with water and left for approximately 20 minutes before paste can be applied. A systematic approach therefore needs to be developed so that while one panel is soaking, another is being applied. It can be a good idea to pencil the timings on the back of the panels, so that you can gauge accurately when each one is ready for pasting.

3 Use the recommended paste on the back of the panels, taking care to ensure that the entire surface has an even coverage of the paste.

Work the brush from the center out to the edges of the panel, and try to avoid getting any paste on the table. Any overspill should be removed with a damp sponge.

4 Apply the first panel to the wall using the pencil guidelines for positioning. Use a paperhanging brush to remove air bubbles, running the brush across the entire panel. The bottom edge of the panel should sit flush along the top of the baseboard.

5 Join subsequent panels using the same technique, butting the edges tightly together. However, take care not to allow any overlaps because these will show up clearly in the finished effect—a slight gap is actually preferable to an overlap.

👍 tips of the trade

Once in position, panels must be primed with an oil-based undercoat before additional coats of paint and decorative effects can be applied.

site-made paneling

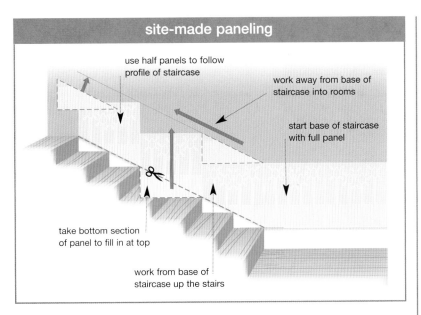

use half panels to follow profile of staircase

work away from base of staircase into rooms

start base of staircase with full panel

take bottom section of panel to fill in at top

work from base of staircase up the stairs

⑨ Finally, caulk all the joints in the paneling to produce a smooth finish and prevent the edges from lifting at a later date. Remove excess caulk with a damp sponge.

⑥ At the stairwell, cut panels vertically in half and continue to apply them up the staircase. Use the paperhanging brush to mold the bottom section of the panel into the staircase profile. Trim any excess along the junction with a knife.

panel. The angle of ascent of the paneling edge should relate directly to the angle of ascent of the staircase. (The diagram above illustrates how these panels should be cut and fitted.)

⑧ To finish the top edge of the paneling, apply a chair rail (see page 98). The rail should slightly overlap the wall covering, so that a neat, precise finish is produced.

⑦ Take the trimmed excess from the bottom section of the panel and butt it at the top of the same

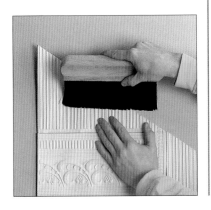

Decorative wall paneling makes an attractive finish in any room, and looks particularly effective when used on stairwells with a matching chair rail.

decorative finishes

However well building tasks have been carried out, the decorative aspect of any renovation work is the deciding factor in determining how good the finished product will look. Therefore, attention to detail at this stage of a project will turn an ordinary finish into an outstanding one. This chapter provides options and instruction on many decorative processes while supplying the crucial information on how to achieve good finishes through thorough preparation and planning. Take time to choose decorative schemes, and use this chapter as a guide for selecting the most appropriate materials and techniques.

Careful thought and planning in terms of color and design will help make the most of your hard work.

choosing finishes

Decoration is very much an issue of personal preference. In general, most people tend to have particular opinions on certain finishes—for example, many people have wallpaper in every room whereas others cannot bear the thought of wallpaper anywhere. Some use strong colors in every room scheme, whereas others shy away to more neutral shades. There is no right or wrong and it can be worth trying out a range of options to find what suits you best.

design aspects

When considering any decorative option, design or period features may influence the type of decoration you use. Both period homes and ultra-modern apartments are similar in this respect, because both have some limitations on the types of materials that can be used if the home is to retain its style or design. Therefore some research on or consideration to authenticity should take part in your final decision-making process.

Converting two rooms into one or widening entrances between rooms is a way of creating a more open-plan layout. While providing a lighter, more spacious atmosphere, consideration needs to be made of the feasibility of removing whole or partial walls, especially if they are load-bearing. However, this sort of renovation can dramatically change the look of your home and totally transform a cramped, rather gloomy atmosphere into a design of far greater appeal.

BELOW *Stripes are an effective wallpaper design and can create the impression of height by making the ceiling appear taller.*

wallpaper

The modern DIY revolution has also increased the range of options open to people who wish to use wallpaper. Manufacturers now produce papers in a greater range of designs, colors, and textures than ever before. Wallpaper has an instant effect, which often makes it an attractive option for many people, but it is important to paint any surrounding woodwork or surfaces in colors that will complement the paper. It's also important to ensure that furnishings in the room will make a suitable contrast or complement to the paper design. Different wallpapers may have markedly different effects on the atmosphere of a room, so choose your pattern carefully.

ABOVE *Period design features, such as fireplaces, can help to create extra interest and provide a focal point in the decorative scheme of a room.*

ABOVE *Tile designs can be used effectively on both walls and floors to create a well-integrated scheme.*

RIGHT *Large, open-plan room designs provide a broad canvas for atmospheric color schemes.*

BELOW *Strong colors are a particularly effective way of picking out the different types of surfaces and features in a room.*

tiles

Tiles form part of the decorative scheme in most bathrooms or kitchens, even if their primary use is for practical purposes. Design choices may be influenced by a desire to tie in colors with other wall decoration, or you may opt for neutral colors that will complement any number of alterations to the surrounding decor.

paint

Paint is the most versatile of all decorative products and is used in most rooms on at least some surfaces. Color availability stretches through every imaginable shade, which means that all tastes are catered to, to the point that there can sometimes be so much choice that it is difficult to decide between closely matched colors. This vastness of range presents plenty of options for coordinating colors and producing complementary or contrasting schemes to suit personal choice.

painting details

Contrasting colors can enliven surfaces, particularly when they are used to pick out certain details or features in a room. The right combinations can create greater texture and add interest to various architectural features. However, the greater the range of colors used, the greater the amount of time that should be spent planning the scheme to ensure that the correct blend is chosen.

choosing materials

Having made decisions on the type of finish you require, it is necessary to choose the best materials for that particular finish. The best materials are those that have the most suitable properties and the right decorative attributes—some finishes are suited to some surfaces more than others, and these factors should be considered before materials are purchased and used.

tiles

Tiles are the most durable decorative material, making them suitable for most areas in the home. Able to withstand bumps and regular cleaning, they are most commonly used in kitchen and bathroom areas.

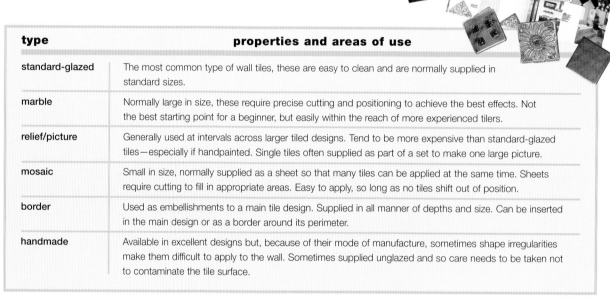

type	properties and areas of use
standard-glazed	The most common type of wall tiles, these are easy to clean and are normally supplied in standard sizes.
marble	Normally large in size, these require precise cutting and positioning to achieve the best effects. Not the best starting point for a beginner, but easily within the reach of more experienced tilers.
relief/picture	Generally used at intervals across larger tiled designs. Tend to be more expensive than standard-glazed tiles—especially if handpainted. Single tiles often supplied as part of a set to make one large picture.
mosaic	Small in size, normally supplied as a sheet so that many tiles can be applied at the same time. Sheets require cutting to fill in appropriate areas. Easy to apply, so long as no tiles shift out of position.
border	Used as embellishments to a main tile design. Supplied in all manner of depths and size. Can be inserted in the main design or as a border around its perimeter.
handmade	Available in excellent designs but, because of their mode of manufacture, sometimes shape irregularities make them difficult to apply to the wall. Sometimes supplied unglazed and so care needs to be taken not to contaminate the tile surface.

wallpaper

Different wallpapers have surprisingly varied properties, which means that they can be used in a range of areas around the home. When choosing a design, do make sure that the actual paper makeup is also suitable.

type	properties and areas of use
lining	Dead flat and available in various thicknesses. Either used as an underlayer for patterned wallpaper or can simply be painted over. Smooths wall surfaces, and provides a softer texture than cold plaster walls.
textured	Relief is built into the paper structure in order to provide pattern and/or texture. Excellent for covering over rough wall surfaces. Some varieties can be painted, while others have a vinyl finish already applied.
standard-patterned	Machine-patterned, and made in vast quantities and ranges of designs. Ideal for most wall surfaces. Often requires lining first, though not on drywall. Available as ready-pasted or paste-the-back varieties.
vinyl	Hardwearing paper designed to be easily cleaned or wiped down. The vinyl layer makes it suitable for bathrooms and kitchens.
natural	Composed of natural fibers, such as silk or hessian. Difficult to hang and best left to the professionals. Provides an outstanding finish, but not particularly durable.

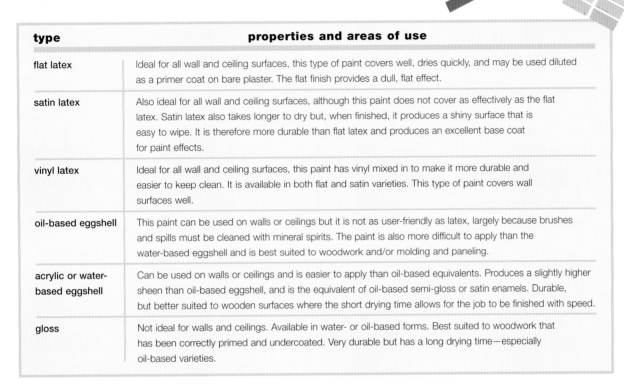

paint

This table contains some of the most common finishing paints for walls and ceilings, and explains their relevant properties. In addition to these common varieties, it is possible to choose specialized finishes.

type	properties and areas of use
flat latex	Ideal for all wall and ceiling surfaces, this type of paint covers well, dries quickly, and may be used diluted as a primer coat on bare plaster. The flat finish provides a dull, flat effect.
satin latex	Also ideal for all wall and ceiling surfaces, although this paint does not cover as effectively as the flat latex. Satin latex also takes longer to dry but, when finished, it produces a shiny surface that is easy to wipe. It is therefore more durable than flat latex and produces an excellent base coat for paint effects.
vinyl latex	Ideal for all wall and ceiling surfaces, this paint has vinyl mixed in to make it more durable and easier to keep clean. It is available in both flat and satin varieties. This type of paint covers wall surfaces well.
oil-based eggshell	This paint can be used on walls or ceilings but it is not as user-friendly as latex, largely because brushes and spills must be cleaned with mineral spirits. The paint is also more difficult to apply than the water-based eggshell and is best suited to woodwork and/or molding and paneling.
acrylic or water-based eggshell	Can be used on walls or ceilings and is easier to apply than oil-based equivalents. Produces a slightly higher sheen than oil-based eggshell, and is the equivalent of oil-based semi-gloss or satin enamels. Durable, but better suited to wooden surfaces where the short drying time allows for the job to be finished with speed.
gloss	Not ideal for walls and ceilings. Available in water- or oil-based forms. Best suited to woodwork that has been correctly primed and undercoated. Very durable but has a long drying time—especially oil-based varieties.

paint effects

Paint effects are produced by the use of a colored glaze that allows for the creation of broken-color finishes on a wall surface. So the materials used are more concerned with achieving pattern and effect, rather than actually containing finishing properties in their own right.

type	properties and areas of use
acrylic or latex glaze	This is water-based, and makes an ideal base for the majority of paint effects. It dries quickly—helping to speed the process but also necessitating speedy application. User-friendly and easy to clean tools after use.
transparent oil glaze	This is oil-based and has similar properties to acrylic or latex glaze, but it may need the addition of turpentine to achieve the correct medium—this varies between manufacturers. It requires a long drying time and is less user-friendly than the acrylic equivalent.
tints	Used to add color to glazes. Some tints are universal in that they may be added to either medium, whereas others are only appropriate for use with one or the other. Only small quantities are required as the pigment is very strong.
varnish	This is used to cover finished effects for protective purposes and allows the surface to be wiped clean. Flat or gloss finishes are available.
glaze coat	Similar to varnish except that it is always water-based. Easy and quick to apply, it produces a surface that is easy to clean. Provides a slight sheen to the finish.

ceiling & wall preparation ↗

The quality of a decorative finish depends on thorough surface preparation. This stage of the renovation procedure is one of the most important in terms of ensuring that the building work you have carried out will be shown off to its best possible potential. It is important not to rush surface preparation and to make sure that any defects are corrected before proceeding in order to prevent their appearance in the final surface.

filling

Filling cracks, joints, or holes in wall and ceiling surfaces is a relatively uncomplicated task, and you will achieve the best results by following a methodical order of work. There are three main types of filler: all-purpose filler, flexible filler, and expandable foam. Each type is designed for a particular kind of task, and all products currently on the market are based on one of these varieties.

all-purpose filler

Manufacturers describe this type of filler as all-purpose, but although it can physically be used for most things, it is still best suited to particular types of holes. It can be bought ready mixed or as a powder to which water is added and a smooth creamy filling paste created. It is most effective in small divots and dents on open wall or ceiling surfaces.

1 Remove any dust in the hole and dampen it slightly to improve the filler's adhesion. Use a putty knife to

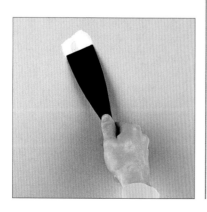

press the filler into place, applying pressure with the knife's flexible blade. Leave the filler slightly raised above the hole—it shrinks slightly as it dries—but remove excess from around the outside.

2 Once dry, sand to a smooth finish, level with the surrounding wall. For deep holes, a second application of filler may be necessary because excessive shrinkage can pull the first application down below the hole surface. Be careful if using a power sander on drywall because it is easy to damage its surface.

flexible filler

Although some all-purpose fillers claim to have flexible qualities, they tend not to achieve the standards set by tubed flexible filler or caulk. This type of filler is used along corner or ceiling junction cracks where slight movement is always prevalent. Although all-purpose filler can be used in these areas, it tends to crack after time, whereas flexible filler or caulk tolerates more stress through movement. However, take care to smooth the filler before it dries, as it is not possible to sand it.

1 Use a caulking gun to apply sealant along the corner cracks, allowing the filler to bead over and cover the crack beneath.

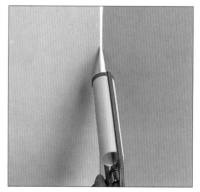

2 Before the filler dries, use a wet finger or a sponge to smooth the filler into the junction. Keep a cup of water handy to wet or clean your finger as you work on shaping the filler.

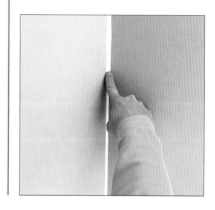

3 For storage purposes, insert a nail or screw into the nozzle of the filler tube to prevent it from hardening in the nozzle and making it difficult to use when next required.

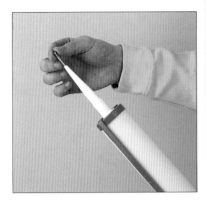

expandable foam

In large gaps or holes, especially around awkwardly shaped inlets such as pipes, the use of flexible or all-purpose filler is neither suitable nor economic. Expandable foam is ideal as it gets into all the small crevices, adheres well, and makes a neat finish. However, it is best to use it with all-purpose filler because expandable foam has a rough texture. So, once the major filling process is complete, finish off the surface with a final skim of all-purpose filler.

Expandable foam is aerosol-based, and is guided into a hole using an extended nozzle. As its name suggests, once out of the aerosol the chemical makeup of the foam expands and takes up the entire area that requires filling. This leads to the foam protruding from the hole. Once dry, this can be trimmed back with a utility knife to a neat finish and then skimmed with all-purpose filler. Be sure to follow the manufacturer's safety guidelines.

caulking blade

A caulking blade or caulker (not to be confused with caulk in terms of flexible filler) is ideal for speeding up the all-purpose filling process. On walls with a number of small holes, draw the wide, filler-loaded blade of the

caulker across the surface. This enables you to fill several holes simultaneously, rather than having to attend to each one separately with a small filling knife.

tips of the trade

Although it is important not to jeopardize the quality of the finish by rushing the job, there are a number of practical, time-saving measures that can be taken. Various tools have been designed to speed up DIY tasks, and electric sanders, in particular, are useful pieces of equipment. Sanding is never the most inspirational or invigorating of tasks and so using an electric sander helps to speed up the process. Be wary, however, of using it directly on drywall. It can damage the surface and the dust can be a health hazard.

cleaning and sealing surfaces

Once the necessary filling and sanding of surfaces has been completed, it is important to clean surfaces with warm water and mild detergent in order to remove dust and impurities. Finally, rinse the surfaces with clean water and allow them to dry. Depending on their condition and what layers are to be applied, it may also be necessary to seal the surfaces before starting to paint or paper over them. Use a suitable primer in order to seal the wall. If you're planning to repaper, apply sizing to achieve a better finished product.

type	surface treatment
surfaces that have been stripped of paper	Must be sealed with a primer
drywalled	Bare drywall primer must be applied to the surface before painting or papering
new plaster	Must be sealed with a primer specified for plaster before painting or papering
old painted	Ensure the surface is completely clean. Sizing is required if paper is to be applied
old papered	Inadvisable to paint over an old papered surface unless you are sure the paper is firmly stuck down
wood paneling	Prime and paint as required, or apply a natural wood finish

painting techniques ↗↗

The quality of a painted finish is dependent on both the type of paint used and the method of application. Therefore, having purchased quality materials, you should develop a good painting technique in order to achieve the best possible finishes. There are a number of different tools that may be used for applying paint, and many are suited to particular surfaces and tasks, but a certain amount of personal preference can also influence your choice.

tools for the job

mini roller tray

mini roller

roller frame

short-pile roller cover

rough-pile roller cover

roller tray

drop cloth

putty knife

long-handled roller

lining brush

roller extension pole

synthetic bristle brushes

dusting brush

paint bucket

natural bristle brushes

brushes

ceilings

Painting ceilings always tends to produce the initial problem of gaining the best access. Although using a stepladder and brush is an option, there are far more efficient and easier ways of going about this task.

1 Attach an extension pole to the roller so that the ceiling can be painted with your feet on the floor. (An extension pole is also useful for painting walls, as it helps gain access to the top area of a wall and reduces the need to bend over for lower wall areas.) Using an extension pole also produces a more even pressure during paint application and improves the quality and evenness of the finish.

2 Having used a roller, you need to finish or cut in around the edges of the ceiling. A brush is the best tool for this purpose. If the walls in the room are to be painted, allow the ceiling color to extend slightly down on to the wall surface—when the wall is painted, you may then paint over the excess ceiling color and cut precisely into the

wall/ceiling junction. This technique ensures that you do not waste time cutting in the ceiling color.

👍

tips of the trade

New equipment is always being devised and, while some people prefer traditional tools, it can be worth experimenting.

improving technique

There are a number of factors that can affect the final appearance of a painted surface. Practicing your painting technique will always help to ensure a good ceiling or wall finish, as will considering the following points.

number of coats

Probably one of the key factors in producing a good finish, it is always best to have a flexible attitude when deciding on coat requirement. As a rule, no surface should receive fewer than two coats of paint and new plaster surfaces should get three. The quality of paint you are using will also determine the requirement—hence the false economy of buying cheap paint. Refreshing a previously painted room with the same color as before will only require one coat. So flexibility is the key but, as a general rule, the greater the number of coats, the better the finish.

wet edges

The chemical makeup of modern paints often includes such substances as vinyl (making them easily washable), which can be a problem when painting. The slight sheen that the vinyl produces can cause highlighting of areas where paint layers are greater than in other areas. This occurs when the central areas of a wall are painted, left to dry, and then the edges cut in later. So as coats are applied, the slight overlap between the edge of the central wall areas and the cut-in edges acquire a buildup of paint layers, which can cause a noticeable color difference. To prevent this, paint one wall at a time so that both the edges and central area of the wall are painted and therefore dry at the same time. This is especially important for dark colors, which can be more noticeable than lighter shades.

roller trails

The texture of rollers leaves a slight imprint in the paint and surface finish. Make sure you avoid paint buildup at the ends of rollers, as this can lead to thicker paint lines or trails on the ceiling or wall surface.

priming

Prime areas that have been filled with an all-purpose filler using your chosen wall color. Otherwise, the varying

absorption properties of the filler and the wall can cause shading differences when additional coats of paint are added.

For troublesome stains on an older painted surface area, it is best to use a ready-made stain sealer to coat the area before continuing with finishing paint.

Where flexible filler or caulk has been used, it is always best to prime it with an oil-based undercoat, as water-based latex applied directly to the caulk can sometimes crack as it dries.

spraying

In some circumstances, a spray gun is a useful tool for painting large open areas. However, always mask off areas that do not require painting, and wear goggles and a respiratory mask. Apply a number of thin coats rather than a few thicker ones, as this will help to prevent runs in the finish.

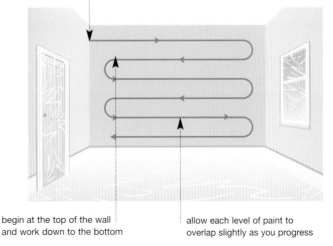

start the gun slightly to the side of the section to be painted and then progress on to the area

begin at the top of the wall and work down to the bottom

allow each level of paint to overlap slightly as you progress

paint effects ⁊⁊

The popularity of paint effects has never been greater and manufacturers are responding to this demand by producing various tools, equipment, and materials. One of the most important materials is the glaze—quality paint effects tend to be as dependent on this as they are on the technique or correct equipment. Some techniques are slightly more difficult than others, so it's worth bearing in mind the level of skill required when choosing which effect to have.

tools for the job

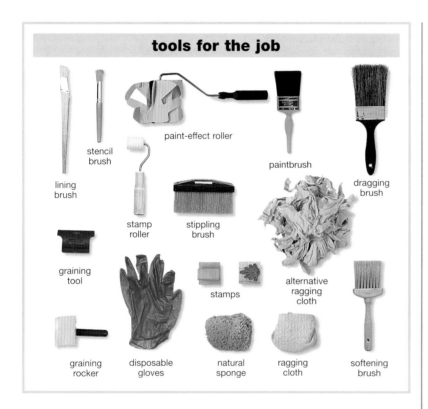

lining brush

stencil brush

paint-effect roller

paintbrush

stamp roller

stippling brush

dragging brush

graining tool

stamps

alternative ragging cloth

graining rocker

disposable gloves

natural sponge

ragging cloth

softening brush

wrong color, which then cannot be mixed back, and so leads to waste.

dilution considerations

Remember that the strength of tint in a small area will considerably be diluted when added to a large quantity of glaze. Therefore, bear in mind that although the pigment of tints is very strong, once applied to the wall there will be some dilution of the effect.

quantities

Directions will vary between manufacturers in terms of how much pigment is required and how much coverage the glaze will provide on the wall surface. Remember, however, that although glaze does go a lot farther than traditional paints do, if you run out it will be nearly impossible to remix a glaze exactly the same. Therefore, always mix up more than you need, to be sure that this situation cannot arise. Any leftover mixture can always be stored in an airtight container for future projects.

mixing colors

Most paint effects are created using transparent glaze. This is the medium that provides the textured or three-dimensional effect that makes paint effects appealing. Traditionalists would argue that the glaze should be oil-based, but by far the most user-friendly glazes are latex-, acrylic-, or water-based equivalents. These can simply be bought off the shelf so that mixing color becomes a basic process of adding pigment or tints to the glaze in order to achieve the shade you require.

However, some caution and instruction is required for this process in order to avoid waste and to be sure

that the color you mix will actually be the color you want on the final wall surface.

adding tints

Before adding color to the glaze, it is first necessary to mix tints to produce the shade you require. It is unlikely that your perfect color requirement will be that of a particular tube of tint, so mixing is nearly always necessary. When you are happy with the shade you have mixed, add some of it to a small quantity of glaze on a mixing palette, so that you can test it on a discrete area of wall or scrap of wood. Skipping this process and adding tint directly to large quantities of glaze can lead to a glaze being mixed to the

techniques

Most paint effects are categorized by whether they involve "on" or "off" techniques. The former involves using a tool to apply the effect directly to the wall, whereas the latter involves applying glaze to the wall with a regular paintbrush before using a tool to apply an effect in the glaze. The same tool may be used in both techniques, but with a completely different finished effect. For example, the finish produced by sponging on is markedly different to that of sponging off. However, not all tools can be used for both methods and some are more clearly suited for one technique or the other.

sponging on

Dip a dampened natural sponge into wet glaze and remove any excess before lightly applying the sponge to the wall surface. Change your wrist angle and sponge direction as you progress across the wall in order to achieve a totally random effect. Wash out the sponge periodically.

ragging off

Apply glaze to the wall with a paintbrush and use a crumpled, dampened rag to make impressions of the rag in the glazed surface. Change your hand angle and the position of the rag to maintain a random effect. Work only in areas of

1yd² (1m²) at a time, otherwise the glaze will dry before you get a chance to make the impressions. Use a new rag (or wash the old one) when it becomes clogged with glaze.

stippling

Apply glaze to the wall before using a stippling brush to make fine, textured imprints in the glaze surface. Keep the bristles of the brush at right angles to the wall surface at all times. Again, only work in areas of 1yd² (1m²) at a time, and remove excess glaze from the bristles at regular intervals.

color washing

Probably the most simple "off" paint effect, color washing involves brushing on the glaze and literally using the texture of the brush to produce the finished effect. Brushstrokes can be used randomly or in a uniform manner, depending on taste. Also, more than one coat may be applied to build up the overall depth of finish.

STAMPING

Stamps (like stencils) provide a method of applying a definite image to a wall surface. The design can be anything decorative and may be combined with other types of paint effects—used on top of them— or applied directly onto plain, painted walls.

● Apply paint to the back face of the stamp using a specially designed foam roller. Test the stamp on scrap paper before applying it to the wall, in order to check for the correct amount of paint to apply for the depth of finish you require.

● Apply the stamp to the wall, ensuring that it does not slip on the wall surface during application and therefore smudge the image. Lift the stamp at a right angle away from the wall surface, and then move on to the next position. Paint can be reapplied between each stamp application or every two to three uses, which helps to produce a softer, more random effect.

wallpapering techniques ⚡

Wallpapering requires a methodical approach, with close attention to detail. It is important to take time when choosing your paper, ensuring that it suits aesthetic requirements and that you will feel confident applying it. Some papers are easier to use than others and subtle patterns can make accurate alignment particularly difficult, but careful practice should make the process easier.

3 Use a utility knife to trim lengths at both ceiling and floor level. For the best results, trim slightly on to the ceiling and baseboard respectively, so that when the paper is brushed into place, the best-looking finish is produced.

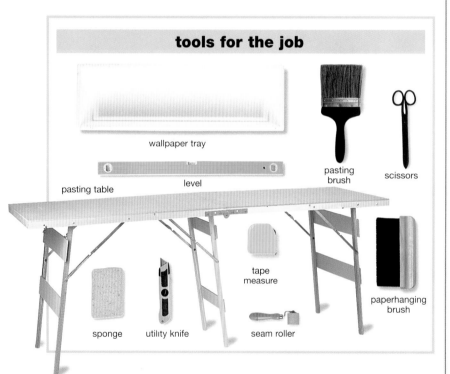

tools for the job

wallpaper tray

pasting brush

scissors

pasting table

level

tape measure

paperhanging brush

sponge

utility knife

seam roller

4 Always butt-join the lengths and make the pattern meet at eye level. It normally follows that the pattern will match along the entire length, but occasionally "pattern drop" does occur. In these instances, it is better to have the best match where the paper is most seen, in other words, at eye level.

Try to decide on a starting point that allows the first length of paper to be a full one—that is to say, the only trimming required will be at the top and bottom edges. The exact starting position will depend on the particular room's shape. With most papers it is best to start near a corner, because if a joint is required it is least noticeable when positioned on a corner junction. With large patterns, the design should be centered on any prominent walls such as a chimney breast, so that a balanced effect will be created.

1 Use a level to draw a vertical line from ceiling to floor—this will provide a guideline for positioning the first length.

2 Apply paste to the back of the first length of paper (if required) and position it so that the edge runs down the vertical guideline. Use a paperhanging brush to remove air bubbles, brushing the paper out from the center toward the edges.

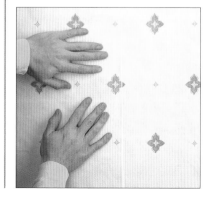

Ceilings are sometimes lined to improve their finish, or they may be wallpapered as an additional decorative option. In both cases, it is important to begin in the correct place and to paper across the longest dimension, thus minimizing the number of joints. Obstacles, such as light fixtures, must also be taken into account. You will need at least two pairs of hands and should pay extra attention to safety:

- Construct a safe access platform from which to work (see page 37)
- Turn off electricity at the main panel when working around electrical fixtures

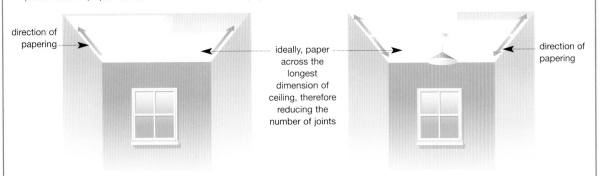

direction of papering

ideally, paper across the longest dimension of ceiling, therefore reducing the number of joints

direction of papering

When papering a ceiling without obstacles such as light fixtures, start against the wall and work across the surface area.

When papering a ceiling with obstacles such as light fixtures, start in the center of the room and work away from the fixture in both directions.

invisible joints

In some circumstances, butt-joining lengths may be impossible. On an outside corner, for example, the length of paper becomes slightly creased because it cannot round the corner and still remain vertical.

1 Allow the length to overlap on to the previous one, matching the pattern on the overlap.

2 Using a utility knife and straightedge—a level is ideal—cut through the center of the overlap from ceiling to floor.

3 Peel back the edges of the full lengths and remove the two strips of excess paper. Then brush the edges back into place to reveal a perfect joint between the two lengths.

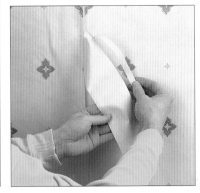

PREPARING TO PAPER

Before applying paper to the walls, it is necessary to run through a few standard checks and procedures.

- **Paper type**—Determine whether the paper is prepasted or whether the back requires paste application. Although the technique for hanging both is similar, the tool and material requirements vary slightly.

- **Lots**—Always check that the rolls display the same lot numbers. This is because there may be a slight shading difference between manufactured lots.

- **Cutting**—When cutting paper, always allow for the size of the pattern repeat and a small excess for trimming purposes at each end.

- **Lining**—Walls should generally be lined with lining paper before wallpaper is applied. Check the manufacturer's guidelines on the particular wallpaper you are using for their recommendations.

tiling techniques

In addition to being decorative, tiles offer a practical wall-covering option. Easy to clean and durable, their use tends to be concentrated in areas such as the kitchen and bathroom. In terms of applying tiles to the wall, in much the same way as wallpapering, emphasis must be put on keeping the tiles level and plumb to ensure a balanced effect. Actual application requires a methodical technique combining meticulous planning as well as accurate measuring and cutting.

PREPARING TO TILE

Before tiling, it is important to be fully prepared, organizing your order of work, to minimize mistakes and confusion.

- **Checking tiles**—Always open boxes of tiles before purchasing to ensure that there are no broken tiles.

- **Shuffling**—When using single-colored tiles for the entire or major part of a design, mix up or shuffle the tiles between boxes so that any slight color variations will be evenly spread across the tiled surface and therefore invisible to the naked eye.

- **Tile gauge**—To help decide on starting points, make a tile gauge from a piece of wooden batten. Lay a line of tiles out dry on a flat surface (allowing for the spacers) and hold a piece of batten along their length. Use a pencil to mark off the joints between the tiles on the batten. Now hold the batten against the wall and use it as a gauge to determine the most suitable position for the tile layout. It also allows you to plan cuts in the most suitable places and for a balanced effect to be achieved.

- **Spacers**—You can buy bags of individual spacers or sheets of spacers that need to be broken up before use. It is best to break up a number of sheets before you begin to tile, so that time isn't wasted when applying tiles to the wall surface.

- **Keeping clean**—Always keep a bucket of clean water on hand so that surfaces and tools can be kept clean at all times.

tools for the job

rod saw

sponge

tile cutter

grout raker

grout shaper

grout spreader

adhesive spreader

tile cutting machine

There are a few simple guidelines that may be applied to most tiling projects.

1 The top of a baseboard is rarely precisely level, nor is it the best point to apply the first row of tiles. Therefore, nail a piece of batten in position above the baseboard using a level as a guide. This will support the tiles and prevent them from slipping down the wall surface. Once the main body of tiles is complete and dry, you can remove the batten and fill the area above the baseboard with cut tiles.

2 Spacers must be used to maintain the distance between tiles, but remove them before grouting or the grout may crack. At the bottom level, they can be positioned flat on

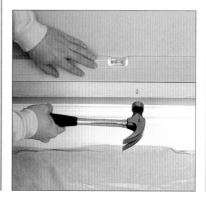

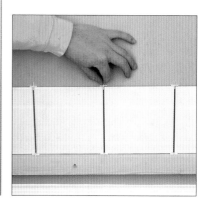

tiling sequence

Although each room differs, there is a basic order of tiling that will help to achieve the best finish.

1 Apply full tiles
2 Fill in around obstacles
3 Complete corners
4 When main design is dry, fill in cut tiles at bottom of wall
5 Apply border tiles if required

1 full tiles

2 fill in around obstacles

5 apply border tiles if required

4 use cut tiles at the bottom of the wall

3 complete corners

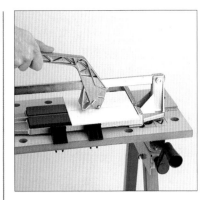

and score along this line to produce a definite scratch through the glazed surface of the tile.

2 Design varies between tile cutters, but the principle of breaking the tile along the scored line involves applying weight to either side of the line, causing it to crack along the cut.

the batten and remain there until the tile adhesive has dried. They may then be removed along with the batten.

3 When grouting, always use a grout spreader or float (never your fingers), moving it in all directions across the tiles to press the grout into every joint. Remove the excess from the tiles as you progress. Never grout more than 20yd² (20m²) at a time so that the grout does not set before you complete step 4.

4 Wipe down the tiled surface with a damp sponge before using a grout shaper to tool the joints and provide a neat finish

to the wall. Run the shaper along the joint to smooth the grout in between the tiles.

cutting tiles

Cuts can be divided into two simple categories—those that are straight and those that have a curve.

straight cuts

1 Although hand-held tile cutters can be used for this purpose, a tile cutting machine is the ideal tool for accuracy and ease of use. Measure the size of the required cut

curved cuts

Cutting curves involves the use of a specially designed rod saw. Clearly mark the curved guideline on the tile and clamp it to a workbench before cutting through the tile using the saw.

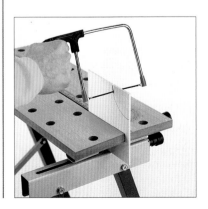

creating a textured ceiling finish ⤢

Various types of finish may be added to flat ceiling surfaces to produce a textured or patterned effect. These coatings can be used on drywalled or plastered ceilings, or even over rougher, wavy surfaces, helping to create a more attractive finish. However, textured coatings should never be applied on top of wallpaper or lining paper, and they must only be applied to ceilings that have been sealed and are therefore stable for accepting this type of coating.

tools for the job

There are specific tools available for creating a textured finish. Not all of these pieces will be required—the tools you use depend upon the the type of texture or pattern you are planning to create (see below).

block brush

standard comb

combination comb

mixing tool

stippler

rough trowel

pattern roller

caulking blade

creases, as such imperfections will affect the ability of the textured finish to adhere to the ceiling properly.

2 Mix the textured coating in a bucket. Follow the manufacturer's instructions regarding the amount of water required to add to the powder. Although the coating can be mixed by hand, it is much easier to use a mixing tool attached to a drill.

stippling a ceiling

Once the coating has been applied to the ceiling, a specific tool is required to create the finish. Combs or trowels may be used, but in this case, a stippler has been employed to produce a stippled ceiling effect.

👍
tips of the trade

If possible work from a sturdy platform (see page 37), moving gradually across the ceiling surface. Stepladders may be used, but this will involve a lot of effort getting up and down.

1 On plasterboard or drywall ceilings, make sure that all the joints between the separate boards are taped with self-adhesive joint tape. Check that the tape is firmly stuck down and that there are no ripples or

TRADITIONAL TAPING

Instead of using self-adhesive tape, you can use standard joint tape, which needs to be soaked in water before use, then applied to the joints between the drywall sheets in a similar way to the tape used above. Some tapes can simply be embedded in wet compound and smoothed on with a drywall knife.

3 Use a caulking blade or drywall knife to apply a band of textured coating over the drywall joints and any nail heads in the ceiling surface. Allow this area to dry thoroughly before coating the rest of the surface.

4 Use a block brush to apply the main coating to the ceiling surface. Apply a thick, even coat to ensure total coverage and a consistent depth. Work in areas of approximately 1yd² (1m²) at a time, in order to prevent the mixture from drying.

tips of the trade

It is a good idea to have two people working on the surface at any one time —as one person applies the coating, the other can use the stippler. This helps to ensure the coating always has a wet edge and that the job is finished at one time, without any dried, patchy areas. It may also pay to practice the technique on a scrap piece of drywall before beginning work on the ceiling. This is especially important when using combs, as the technique can take time to master.

5 Take the stippler and press it into the surface coating at a right angle to the ceiling. Lift away, again at a right angle to the surface, and move to the adjacent coated area. Overlap the stippled impressions slightly to produce a random effect. Change the angle of the face of the stippler on the surface for an even greater random effect. Repeat steps 4 and 5 across the ceiling surface until the whole area is complete.

6 Finish off around the ceiling edge by dampening a 1in (2.5cm) brush and drawing it through the wet coating. This provides a neat border to the coating.

tips of the trade

Once dry, textured coatings can be left uncoated, but you can add a flat or satin finish if you prefer.

These coatings provide an effective finish on a ceiling, giving depth and texture to what is normally a flat, rather two-dimensional area in a room.

repair & restoration

Not all construction projects involve the complete rebuilding of ceilings and walls. Indeed, most jobs are concerned with repairs and alterations to small areas, such as restoring surfaces and areas of damage. This type of work is often quick to carry out but nevertheless important in maintaining or restoring the appearance of walls and ceilings. This chapter covers many of the more common repair projects that occur around the house and provides instruction on the best means of dealing with damaged areas. Many of the methods used have been briefly mentioned in earlier chapters, but slight variations are often required when it comes to finding the best techniques for repairs.

Whether painted or stained, tongue and groove provides an attractive and hardwearing finish, to an entire room.

making minor repairs ↗

When preparing to paint or finish a room, it is almost certain that some minor repairs or surface improvement will be required, regardless of the age of the ceiling or wall. All minor imperfections in such surfaces are relatively quick to repair but make an important contribution to the overall look of the room.

ceilings

tools for the job

hammer
nail set
putty knife
utility knife
caulking blade
drywall knife
lining brush

Ceilings tend to avoid a lot of the wear and tear that walls receive because they are, quite simply, out of the way of much traffic and potential damage. However, they do suffer damage from actions such as vibration—often caused by footsteps on the floor above. In many cases this never causes a problem, but sometimes persistent vibration can lead to minor damage in the ceiling surface.

popping nail heads

Nail heads can emerge from the ceiling surface for a number of reasons. In old ceilings, it may be because the nail was not hammered in properly and it has loosened over the years. However, the problem is more common in recently plastered ceilings and indicates that either the plasterboard has not been secured firmly enough— which leads to a slight movement of the board itself—or that the nail is not inserted in a joist properly. The cure for either problem is very simple.

1 Hammer in the nail head slightly below surface level. Alternately, if the nail is loose, remove it with pliers and insert another into the same joist a few inches away.

2 Use joint compound to cover the hole. Allow the compound to dry and sand to a smooth finish.

ceiling cracks

As with popping nail heads, cracks can appear in both old and relatively new ceilings. The tendency is for cracks to follow the joint edges of the drywall sheets, which means that they are normally fairly straight and uniform in their course. However, this is not an exact rule, and cracks may appear for any number of reasons. In minor instances, use joint compound.

1 Use a utility knife to cut along each edge of the crack, removing loose material and shaping the crack into a small valley, or fissure.

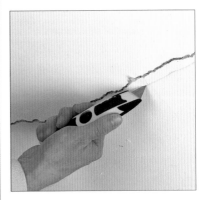

2 Use a putty knife to press joint compound into the crack, resting the edges of the putty knife on either side to produce an even finish. For deep cracks, more than one application may be required. Allow to dry, then sand to a smooth finish.

PERSISTENT CRACKING

Sometimes, no matter how much filling is carried out, small hairline cracks will reappear in ceiling surfaces. Lining the ceiling can help to prevent the cracks from becoming visible, but if they crack the paper as well there may be structural problems, so seek professional advice.

walls

Walls do have the nail popping and cracking problems experienced by ceilings, but they are also prone to other damage as a result of general wear and tear. Again, most can be solved in a relatively short time.

dents and divots

Small dents and scrapes are commonplace on most wall surfaces and are basically unavoidable. It is important that you repair any such marks before painting, to ensure a good finish.

1 For small holes, simply dust out any loose material and use a putty knife to apply joint compound to the area. Allow to dry, then sand to a smooth finish.

2 For larger holes, use the broad face of a caulking blade to apply the joint compound. For deep holes, try more than one application.

peeling tape

On finished walls (or ceilings) the tape used on joints may occasionally work loose and lead to a bulge in the wall surface. This may be because the tape was not secured in place properly during wall construction, or it could simply be a sign of age. Whichever the case, you will need to repair the damage before painting can take place.

1 Tear back the defective area of tape and use a utility knife to cut it away at the place where there is still good adhesion between the tape and jointed wall surface.

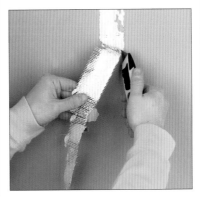

2 Reapply a section of self-adhesive joint tape to the damaged area, following the same procedure as before.

3 Use a drywall knife to spread joint compound along and over the joint. Allow it to dry before sanding the surface to a smooth finish with some sandpaper.

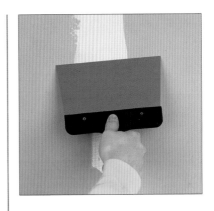

wall & ceiling joint

The joint between the wall and ceiling is another area that can be prone to cracking. To repair standard joints, use flexible filler or caulk as shown on page 108. Ornate joints such as cornice require more work.

1 Apply filler to the damaged area with your finger, making the filler sit slightly above the profile.

2 Use a wet lining brush to mold the filler into position. Allow to dry, then sand gently.

improving ceilings ⫻

Making sure that a ceiling has a good surface for decorating may require more work than simply minor repairs. Severely sagging old ceilings can require demolition and reconstruction (see page 66) but some surfaces have other potential options. For example, applying a new plaster skim over a rough ceiling surface is one way of restoring it to a flatter finish. Alternately, the projects considered below may be more appropriate to your needs.

repair & restoration

124

old textured ceilings

Textured ceilings suit some people more than others. For this reason, you may find it desirable to restore a textured or patterned ceilling back to a flat surface. One technique for removing textured coatings is to use a wallpaper stripper. However, when using such appliances, pay close attention to the manufacturer's operating instructions and adhere to all the required safety procedures—goggles and gloves are essential protective equipment when scraping off high points on a textured ceiling.

Alternately, if the coating is firmly stuck to the ceiling surface, it can be easier and less time-consuming to simply plaster over the top of it. To do this, refer to the plastering techniques described in chapter 5, but you may also need to adopt the refining technique described below.

tools for the job

scraper

large paintbrush or pasting brush

plastering trowel

mixing equipment

1 Use a scraper to knock off all the high points from the textured coating. The degree to which you have to do this will depend on the depth of finish, but generally, removing as much texture as possible will make the plastering process much easier later on.

2 Brush a coat of bonding agent on to the textured surface to seal it and stabilize it in readiness for the plaster.

3 Mix up plaster (see page 87) and apply it to the ceiling with

a plastering trowel. A fairly thick coating of plaster is required in order to take up the roughness or texture on the ceiling, so two coats of plaster may be needed.

THE TEXTURED OPTION

On badly cracked or rough ceilings, there is an option to use textured paint to help take up the roughness or unevenness of the ceiling surface. The texture produced is not the finish of standard textured coatings, but it is enough to fill minor cracks and provide a more even-looking finish, without going to the expense or time of replastering. Bear in mind that plastering a ceiling is by no means a job for a beginner and so textured paint is a serious and economical option for people with less experience.

using textured paper on ceilings

Just as lining paper can be used to smooth a ceiling surface, textured paper can be used to add pattern and interest to the ceiling surface.

The structure of this type of paper is three-dimensional, so some care is required when hanging it. It may be necessary to line the ceiling first to achieve the best possible results.

1 Use a chalk line to gain a precise guideline across the ceiling surface. Secure the paper in the wall/ceiling joint, making sure that the edge of the length runs precisely along the chalk line.

2 Brush out the paper in the usual manner, applying enough pressure to secure it in position and to remove bubbles from beneath, but not so much pressure that the

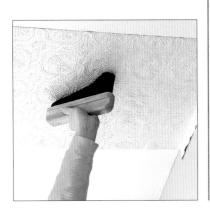

pattern texture becomes crushed. Continue along the length to the other end.

3 Draw a guideline along the wall/ceiling joint, peel the length back, and cut along the guideline with a utility knife or scissors. Once trimmed, brush the end of the paper back in place and repeat the process at the other end of the length.

4 When joining lengths, be careful not to crush the relief with the brush. Wipe off excess paste from the wall and paper surfaces as you work.

Textured paper offers a uniform, patterned finish that gives a greater focus to the ceiling and helps to conceal an uneven surface.

patching a ceiling

Ceiling damage is often caused by basic accidents—the removal of a floorboard, for example, followed by a misplaced foot. The damage can appear catastrophic, but repair is fairly straightforward. Even though ceiling structure itself may vary, the technique for repairing and filling a large area of damage remains the same. Essentially, the affected area must be patched with plasterboard or drywall before finishing with plaster or paint.

tools for the job

stud finder
level or straightedge
pencil
drywall saw
utility knife
claw hammer
cordless drill/driver
hand saw
drywall knife
plastering trowel

1 Use a stud finder to help determine the exact position and direction of the ceiling joists. Alternately, if the hole is very large, you may be able to insert your hand carefully through the gap and feel for the joists that way.

2 Use a straightedge (such as a level) and pencil to mark the area on the ceiling that will need patching. Create a neat, easy-to-cut shape, such as a rectangle. The dimensions should clearly be larger than the hole, and should also extend

to the center of the joists on either side of the hole.

3 Cut through the drywall or plasterboard using a drywall saw. Along the joists it may be necessary to use a utility knife.

4 Use a hammer to remove any nails that are protruding from the joists. The wooden surfaces should be

safety advice

When cutting into a ceiling, check that there is no plumbing or wiring in the area of your work, and be aware of lead and asbestos hazards (page 12).

as level as possible, to ensure that no obstructions will impede the insertion of the new ceiling patch.

5 Cut two lengths of 2 x 4in (2.5 x 10cm) sawn softwood to act as blocking on either side of the hole. Make sure that they are a tight fit, and use a hammer to ease them into place so that they extend into the ceiling space, while still leaving half the block visible along the cut edge of the hole.

6 Angle in screws at the corners of the blocks so that the screws go through into the existing ceiling joists, securing the blocks firmly into place. It is best to drill pilot holes

before inserting the screws, so as not to apply too much pressure to the blocks and risk pushing them farther into the ceiling space.

7 Cut a piece of plasterboard or drywall slightly less than the dimensions of the hole. Ensure that

tips of the trade

Another key cause of ceiling damage can be from the aftermath of a flood. Where water runs down through floor levels, it soaks the plaster sheeting, breaking it down, and eventually resulting in an entire area breaking away. The repair procedure is the same as that demonstrated here, but some additional attention needs to be given to the painting procedure. This is because water damage causes staining and if you apply water-based paint directly over a stain (even if it has totally dried out), the stain will continue to show through. It is therefore advisable to paint over the patch and surrounding area with an oil-based undercoat, before applying further coats of a water-based acrylic finish. This will help to seal the mark and prevent the stain from reappearing.

the material you use is the same thickness as the existing ceiling. Fasten it in place using drywall nails along the joists and the blocks. To finish a drywall patch, see page 84. Otherwise, proceed to step 8.

8 If finishing with plaster, fill along the joints between the new patch and the surrounding ceiling surface with bonding coat plaster. Be sure to press the bonding coat firmly into the joint so that there are no gaps between the new section of plaster-board and the existing ceiling surface.

9 Mix up some multifinish plaster and apply it to the patch using a plastering trowel. Try to bring the plaster level down to the same level as the ceiling, feathering the edges of the patch to match the surrounding area. Running a dampened paintbrush over the area of plaster that will extend on to the ceiling surface may help to smooth the finish and provide a better surface to sand once the plaster has dried out. When finishing off the new plaster

skim, remember regularly to wet the blade of the plastering trowel as you smooth the surface before allowing it to dry.

Also remember that if the difference to be made up between the new drywall patch and the existing ceiling level is greater than $\frac{1}{8}$ in (3mm), it is better to apply two thin coats of plaster rather than one thick coat. This is because during the drying process, a thick coat of plaster is likely to sag under its own weight, resulting in a very noticeable patch repair area.

PREPARING TO DECORATE

To achieve a good finish and make the patch as unnoticeable as possible, there are a few final procedures that will improve its "invisible" effect.

- Fine sanding—Although a standard procedure for preparation, sanding is even more vital when trying to blend in a ceiling patch. The application of some fine filler, followed by more sanding, will improve the smooth nature of the final finish.

- Patch painting—When painting a patch, even if you are using an identical color to that of the rest of the ceiling, the patch will invariably still show up against the rest of the ceiling surface. It is therefore best to prime the patch, apply a first coat of finishing paint, and then apply the top coat over the patch and across the rest of the ceiling. This may sound extravagant, but it will make the patch less noticeable in the overall finish.

- Lining—The best option is to line the ceiling after the patch repair. The thickness of the lining paper (1000–1200 microns is ideal) helps to smooth the ceiling surface further and reduces the likelihood of patch repairs remaining apparent. Once lined, the ceiling may be painted in the usual way.

making hollow wall repairs ⤴

Hollow walls are found in houses of all ages—modern homes often contain stud walls while older properties tend to have walls constructed of lath and plaster. In both cases, there is a void inside the wall that can cause problems when it comes to effecting a repair. When filler or plaster is applied to a hole in the outer drywall or lath-and-plaster layer, it tends to fall directly into the wall void unless some kind of support can be provided until it dries.

minor lath repairs

In older properties with lath-and-plaster walls, areas of plaster can sometimes work loose from the wooden lath and fall away from the wall. Broken lath can also cause plaster to crumble away, so repair to the lath is required before replastering can begin.

tools for the job

utility knife
dusting brush
aviation snips
screwdrivers
plastering trowel
gauging trowel

1 Trim around the edge of the hole with a utility knife. Carefully remove all the loose material until you get back to an edge where the plaster is still firmly bonded to the lath.

2 Use a dusting brush and vacuum to clean down the lath, removing any dust and debris from its

surface. Pay particular attention to the bottom edge of the hole, where debris tends to collect.

3 Use aviation snips to cut a piece of wire mesh to the size of the hole. Screw it firmly into the lath. It may be easier to drill pilot holes in the lath before inserting the screws.

4 Dampen the hole with bonding agent and apply plaster bonding coat to the hole, pressing it in place with a plastering trowel. Score the surface of the bonding coat with the edge of a gauging trowel. Ensure that the level of the bonding coat sits slightly below the level of the surrounding wall.

5 Once the bonding coat has dried, mix and apply some one-coat plaster to the patch, pressing and smoothing it in position, again with a plastering trowel. Allow it to dry before sanding to a smooth finish with some fine-grit sandpaper. You can then repaint the wall in the usual way.

👍 tips of the trade

As an alternative to one-coat plaster, multifinish may be used. However, one-coat plaster has a slight texture, so it tends to produce a finish similar to the older lath-and-plaster walls. Multifinish plaster, on the other hand, is much smoother and corresponds to the texture of modern finishing plaster.

stud wall repairs

Stud walls require a slightly different technique to that employed for lath and plaster, but again the emphasis is on providing support for the filler while it dries.

1 Square off and cut around the edge of the damaged area with a utility knife. For thick drywall, it may be necessary to use a drywall saw for this process.

2 Cut a scrap piece of drywall to a size slightly larger than the cut hole in the wall. Drill a small hole at the center of the piece of drywall and thread a doubled-over length of string

through the hole. On one side of the drywall, tie the string to a nail to prevent it from coming out of the hole.

3 On the opposite side of the nail, apply some all-purpose adhesive around the edge of the piece of drywall.

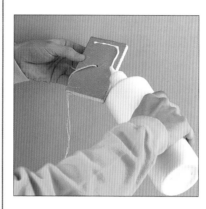

4 Push the drywall through the hole in the wall. Hold on to the length of string with your other hand so that the drywall does not fall into the void.

5 Carefully maneuvering and pulling on the string, position the drywall patch so that it is held firmly up against the hole inside the wall, allowing the adhesive to adhere to the inner edge of the hole. Tie off the

👍

tips of the trade

Dealing with surface damage is demonstrated on page 122, but if damage extends into the cavity of the wall, a different system is required.

string on a piece of scrap wood, thus holding the patch in position while it dries.

6 Once the adhesive has dried, remove the batten and cut the string. Use all-purpose filler to fill the hole—you will need more than one application for a good finish.

Large holes

For larger holes than those demonstrated here, it is possible to employ the technique used to repair ceiling damage (see pages 126–7). In other words, trim the damaged area back to the vertical studs in the wall, creating a rectangular hole. Insert blocking horizontally along the top and bottom edge of the hole. Cut some drywall to fill the gap, nail it in place, and finish in the usual way. The technique can be used on any holes that require filling—even old entrances. Simply insert studs and blocks as required, before fitting drywall and finishing.

making solid wall repairs ⚒⚒⚒

In many ways, solid wall repairs are easier to carry out than equivalent damage in hollow walls. This is because you do not need to worry about providing support while the plaster or filler dries. However, it can still be challenging to produce a finish that blends with the surrounding wall area. Whether the damaged wall is brick, stone, or block based, the same technique may be used for repair.

tools for the job

hand sledge
cold chisel
protective gloves
safety goggles
dusting brush
old paintbrush
gauging trowel
plastering trowel and float

1 Remove any loose debris from the hole. Use a hand sledge and cold chisel to knock off any rough areas of old base coat or plaster. Always wear safety equipment such as goggles and gloves during this process to protect yourself from bits of debris that tend to fly away from the wall surface.

2 Use a dusting brush and vacuum to clean out the hole as thoroughly as possible. Pay particular attention to the area around the edges, where dirt and dust tend to collect. Before any work can begin, all loose material must be cleared away so that the hole is totally dust free.

3 Mix up some bonding agent and use an old paintbrush to apply the solution liberally in the hole. Again, pay particular attention to the edges of the hole, allowing the solution to extend slightly on to the surrounding wall.

4 Mix up some bonding-coat plaster, and press it firmly into the hole using a gauging trowel. Be sure that the bonding coat is molded into all areas of the hole, and that it is brought up to a level slightly below that of the surrounding wall surface. You may find it easier to combine use of the gauging trowel with a plastering float to ensure an even surface finish.

5 Before it dries, score the surface of the bonding coat using the edge of the gauging trowel. At the same time, make sure that none of the bonding coat is pushed above wall level, as this will affect the finish when you apply the top plaster coat.

👍 tricks of the trade

If you do not have bonding-coat and multifinish plaster, it is possible simply to build up the patch with layers of one-coat plaster. This will not produce the same totally smooth, even finish as that of multifinish plaster, but its slightly rougher surface may be more appropriate on the less smooth wall surfaces of very old houses.

6 Mix up and apply a coat of multifinish plaster, using a plastering trowel to press it firmly into position. For holes of this size, rest the edges of the plastering trowel on the wall surrounding the hole, enabling you to produce a neat finish.

7 This finish can be further leveled by cutting a length of batten to slightly longer than the hole diameter and gradually drawing the batten across the plaster surface, again making it as level with the surrounding wall as possible.

9 Smooth, or polish, the plaster patch with the wet trowel until a totally even and level finish is achieved. Once the plaster dries, a light sanding will be necessary to smooth the surface before you can paint it.

HOLE TYPES

• **Deep holes**—Where depth is greater than that shown above, it is necessary to apply a base coat to the hole before plaster can be applied. As always, it is better to apply thin layers rather than trying to speed up the process with thicker ones. Over-application simply causes the base coat or plaster to bulge and makes it impossible to achieve a smooth finish when applying subsequent coats.

• **Shallow holes**—Where the top layer of plaster has blown away from the layers underneath, it may only be necessary to apply a single finishing coat. In such cases, however, it is common to find that if one area of top layer plaster has come away, this may be the case for most of the rest of the wall surface. Tapping the surface with the butt end of a trowel and listening for hollow reverberations will give some indication of the stability of the surface. If the plaster is indeed loose, it is better to remove and replaster at this stage rather than repaint and face a similar patching problem in the near future.

8 Allow the plaster to dry slightly. Then use an old paintbrush to wet the surface of a plastering trowel with some clean water.

👍

tricks of the trade

Plastering is always a messy job, so it is important to keep surfaces and tools clean at all times. When applying plaster or base coat to a hole, keep a clean sponge handy so that you can wipe away any excess material that gets on the surrounding wall surface. It is always better to clean such messes off the wall while they are still wet—if the base coat or plaster is allowed to dry, their removal will be much more difficult and may require a combination of sanding and scraping to attain a flat surface.

FINISHING OFF

• **Drying naturally**—The temptation when patching a small area of wall is to try to force the drying process by applying heat directly to the patch. This can have the effect of cracking the base coat and plaster, which will then require additional repair in order to achieve the desired finish. Cracking can be avoided by allowing the patch to dry naturally at room temperature.

• **Priming**—Once dry, ensure that the newly plastered area is primed before additional coats of paint are applied. Use a primer specified for use on plaster for this purpose.

• **Lining option**—On walls that may have a number of patch repair requirements, it may be necessary to consider lining the wall after repairs are complete, in order to smooth the surface further. On particularly uneven walls, woodchip or textured paper is another possibility for providing a more even wall finish.

repairing corners 🔨🔨🔨

Damaged inside corners can be treated in a similar way to open wall surfaces (see page 128)—plaster or filler is simply worked up to the corner junction and smoothed in place as required. However, outside corners require slightly more work as there is a need to restore the profile of the corner itself. There are two main methods for carrying out this sort of repair, depending upon the extent or depth of the damage along the outside corner itself.

minor corner repairs

Where a corner has been damaged in a small area, it should be quite simple to restore the profile and sharp edge. It's worth bearing in mind that wall structure is not an important consideration because the same technique may be used on solid-block or stud walls.

tools for the job

hand saw

hammer

putty knife

1 Cut a length of wood batten, slightly longer than the length of the damaged corner section. The width of the batten should also be greater than the width of the widest point of damage on either of the two walls that meet to form the corner. Nail the batten in place on one wall, allowing its edge to run precisely down the corner edge. Make sure the nails can be removed easily later.

2 Mix up some high-strength joint compound, employing a putty knife to press it firmly into the corner hole. Use the wall on one side and batten on the other to rest the edges of the knife, thereby creating a flush finish over the hole surface.

3 Let the compound dry, remove the batten, and reposition it on the adjacent wall running precisely down the corner edge. Fill the hole as required, bringing the compound up to and slightly over the level of the batten and surrounding wall surface.

4 Let the compound dry, remove the batten, and sand the corner to a smooth, sharp edge. You will need to fill and sand the holes made by the nails when attaching the batten. If required, use some fine surface filler as a final measure to smooth any indentations not covered by the initial compound application.

complete corner repairs

Where damage is consistent along the complete length of a corner, it is better to repair the entire corner, rather than repairing small areas. In this case you need to make a more mechanical repair using corner bead to help restore the corner profile.

tools for the job

hacksaw

gauging trowel

plastering trowel

1 Cut corner bead to the required corner length using a hacksaw. (Tin snips or side cutters may be used but a hacksaw tends to produce a neater and more accurate cut.)

$\textcircled{2}$ Mix a small amount of multifinish plaster, making sure it is a firm consistency. Apply the plaster with a gauging trowel along the edge of the corner at approximately 12in (30cm) intervals.

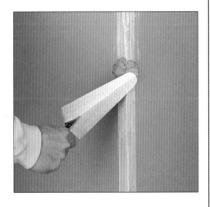

$\textcircled{3}$ Press the length of corner bead into position along the outside corner edge. Allow the plaster to squeeze through the mesh of the bead, so that there is good contact between the bead and the corner.

$\textcircled{4}$ Use the edge of the trowel to remove excess plaster from the front surface of the bead. Make any

final adjustments in the bead position to ensure that it is vertical and running directly along the corner junction.

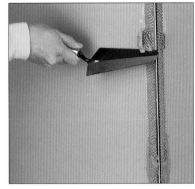

$\textcircled{5}$ Once the plaster has dried and the bead is anchored in position, mix up some more multifinish plaster and use a plastering trowel to apply it in a wide band along each corner edge. Use the metal edge of the corner bead to help guide the trowel down the wall surface, keeping an even coat of plaster covering the entire corner area. Apply a wide band to feather in the new plaster level with the existing wall surface. (This is because applying plaster directly along the corner—and nowhere else—would provide an unrealistic appearance along its edge.)

freehand corners

Although most outside corners have a precise and rather sharp edge to them, in older houses this is often not the case, and a more rounded finish is clearly apparent. When repairing such corners, the precise apex to the corner is not necessarily required.

tools for the job

plastering trowel

outside corner trowel

$\textcircled{1}$ Use a plastering trowel to apply the plaster along the corner, molding it into position along the corner edge.

$\textcircled{2}$ Use an outside corner trowel to run down the edge of the corner, making an even but not completely sharp edge to the corner. Wetting the trowel with clean water can make this process easier.

repairing wood trim

Wood trim often needs repair and requires different techniques of restoration from those for walls or plaster surfaces. Wood, whether in the form of paneling, baseboard, or any other feature, tends to suffer from general wear and tear such as bumps, scrapes, and splits. Minor faults can be treated with filler, but more serious damage may require replacement sections of wood in order to restore the surface to an attractive finish.

baseboards

The function of baseboard is to add a finish at the wall/floor joint, and to protect the base of the wall from any damage. Unsurprisingly, the baseboard itself can become damaged over time and in need of repair. For short sections of damaged board, the most economical technique is to replace the entire length. However, on long stretches of baseboard this can be seen as wasteful, and inserting a replacement section is better.

tools for the job

pry bar & protective gloves
miter box
hand saw
hammer
tape measure
utility knife
nail set

1 Score along the caulk joint between the baseboard and wall surface with a utility knife, then

ease the baseboard away from the wall using a pry bar. (Wear protective gloves for this process.) Position two pieces of batten behind the baseboard and wedge the board free of the wall surface.

2 Position a miter box in front, and to one side, of the damaged section of baseboard. Cut down through the baseboard with a hand saw. Move the miter box to the other side and then cut on the opposite miter angle through the baseboard. Remove the damaged section.

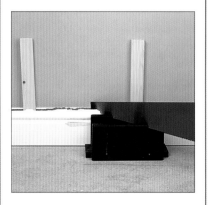

3 Nail the baseboard back in position on either side of the gap you have created. Take accurate

measurements for the new piece of baseboard you require and cut a length to fit, remembering to miter each end to fit snugly in the gap.

4 Before securing in place, test to see that your new section fits. Then apply some wood glue along the cut edge of the new piece and position it, removing any excess adhesive with a damp cloth.

5 Attach the section permanently by nailing finish nails through the mitered joint at either end of the new section of baseboard. Three nails along each side should be sufficient. Set the nail heads in before painting the baseboard.

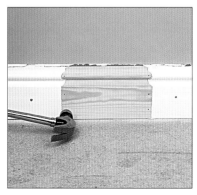

repairing tongue and groove

Damaged tongue-and groove-paneling presents a different set of problems because removing the panels—which have blind fasteners—can be tricky. Some ingenuity is therefore required so that the damaged boards can be replaced without causing damage to the surrounding panels.

tools for the job

cordless drill

keyhole saw

pry bar

claw hammer or pliers

hand saw

wooden mallet

chisel

1 Drill a hole to the side of the damaged tongue-and-groove board and along the joint it makes with the adjacent board. Choose a drill bit large enough to accommodate a keyhole saw.

2 Use a keyhole saw to cut through the joint. Work up and down along the joint, until total separation between the two lengths has been achieved. Accuracy is not vital as the aim is simply to gain access to the damaged board in order to make your repair.

3 Use a pry bar to lever out the damaged board. You may also need to work a little on the other side of the board, because there will be other nails holding the panel in place. However, with one edge loose, a combination of levering and easing should result in the board coming free. It is also worthwhile to remove the board adjacent to the broken one, as the damage caused during cutting is likely to be noticeable.

4 After both boards have been removed, use a claw hammer or pliers to take out any nails that may still be present in the exposed battens

beneath the tongue-and-groove paneling. Failure to remove them will hinder progress later.

5 Cut two new lengths of tongue and groove to size. Use a mallet and chisel to trim the tongue off one of the lengths—this is because damage caused in removing the old lengths may have affected the actual interlocking mechanism of the tongue-and-groove system. By removing the tongue on one length, it should then be possible to insert the strip into the existing paneling.

6 Interlock the two new sections into the paneling, and secure them in place with finish nails. The new paneling may then be primed and painted.

tips of the trade

Tongue and groove is supplied in a range of thicknesses, so always check your requirements before purchasing replacement strips.

glossary

Baseboard—decorative wooden molding applied at base of wall.

Base coat or scratch coat—mortar-based coat used as undercoat for plaster on interior solid block walls. On exterior walls it may be used to form the finished surface.

Block—small length of wood used in ceiling, wall, and floor structure to strengthen joist framework.

Bonding agent—all-purpose adhesive used to bind and/or stabilize surfaces. Used in concentrated and dilute forms.

Casing—decorative wood surround applied around door and window frames or entrances to create finish.

Caulk—flexible filler supplied in a tube and dispensed from a caulking gun. Must be smoothed to finish before it dries. Normally latex acrylic or water-based.

Cavity wall—wall composed of two layers. In effect two walls separated by a cavity or void. Common in construction of exterior walls of modern homes.

Chair rail—wooden rail or molding that divides the wall surface into a lower and upper area.

Common wall—shared wall that divides two properties.

Corner bead—metal, right-angled strip used to create a sharp profile for outside corners before joint compound or plaster is applied.

Cove—decorative molding applied at wall/ceiling joint.

Crown molding—decorative molding applied at wall/ceiling joint. Generally more ornate and of greater depth than cove.

Cutting in—term describing painting in the corners or at the different joints on a wall surface or between walls and ceilings.

Door jamb—wood stock used to make up the interior part of a door frame.

Drywall or wallboard—gypsum layer compressed and sandwiched between thick paper and manufactured in sheets to be used as standard building board for finishing.

Drywalling—referring to the technique of combining drywall and joint compound to create a wall ready for painting or papering. Joint compound is used to cover the area between sheets of drywall.

Eggshell—durable paint that has a dull, flat finish. It is available in both latex acrylic or solvent-based forms.

Glaze—a medium that tints are added to in order to create paint effects. Latex acrylic or solvent-based alternatives.

Hearth—area in front of and at the base of a fireplace.

Inside corner—the corners that point away from the center of the room.

Joint compound—along the lines of plaster, this is used to join gaps between drywall when finishing.

Joint tape—tape used to join drywall sheets before finishing. Self-adhesive varieties available.

Joist—length of wood used in construction of ceilings and floors.

Joist hanger—metal bracket used to bear the weight and position of joist ends in ceiling structure.

Latex or acrylic—or water-based. Term that is used when referring to the makeup of paint or glaze.

Lath—wooden lath are lengths of wood used in the makeup of old walls before the invention of plasterboard. Plaster lath are small plasterboard sheets.

Lining—term referring to the use of lining paper being applied to wall surfaces.

Chair rail: these rails are traditionally used to prevent chairs from damaging the wall surface.

joint tape

Lintel—supportive structure inserted above windows, doors, or openings in masonry walls.

Main panel—box in which electrical cables are joined together.

Master suite—term for a bathroom that is directly adjacent to and serving one particular room. Normally created through building a stud partition wall in a larger room to provide space.

MDF—or medium-density fiberboard. Wood-based building board made from compressed wood fibers.

Miter—angled joint, involving two lengths joining at a right angle and therefore each piece requiring to be cut at a 45-degree angle.

Molding—decorative length of plaster, poly-urethane, or wood used as a decorative detail on wall or ceiling surfaces.

Needle brace—length of wood inserted through a hole in a load-bearing wall to support the weight of the wall before the lintel is positioned. Needle is held in place by steel or wood props at either end.

Niche—molded plaster feature, built or inserted into a wall to make a display area.

Open plan—home design where rooms are spacious, or where smaller rooms have been connected into one large one.

Outside corner—the corners that stick out into the room.

OSB—or oriented strand board. Flooring that is made out of compressed and oriented wood chips, and supplied in sheets. Sheets normally joined with tongue-and-groove mechanism.

Picture rail—wooden molding positioned on upper part of wall. Traditionally used to hang pictures from. Now mainly used as purely decorative feature to break up a wall surface.

Niche: a decorative plaster feature, built into a shallow wall recess, often used to display flowers, ornaments, or statues.

Plasterboard—plaster layer that is compressed and enclosed or sandwiched between thick paper and manufactured in sheets to be used as standard building board for plaster surfaces.

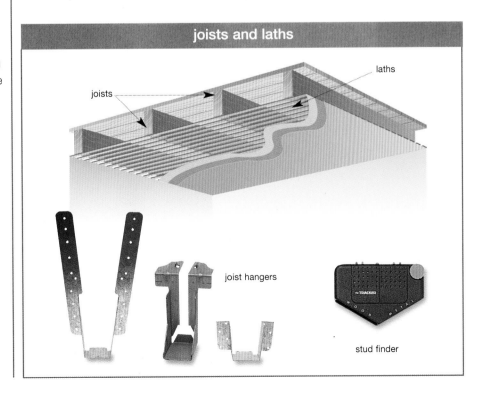

joists and laths

joists

laths

joist hangers

stud finder

Plasticizer—a mortar additive that makes mortar easier to use and work with.

Plywood—thin veneers of wood bonded together to create building board. The grain of alternate layers or veneers tends to run at right angles to one another.

Polishing—referring to technique of finishing a plastered surface with a plastering trowel or float.

Resilient channel—metal strip attached to walls or joists, onto which drywall is fixed. Allows fasteners to attach drywall directly to bar and not to wall, and therefore helps to reduce noise transferal through floors, ceilings, or walls.

Rose—plaster accessories used as ornate ceiling decoration.

Sand pugging—technique of soundproofing where sand is introduced into a floor space in order to insulate and reduce noise traveling between floors.

Scrim—traditional type of joint tape used to cover joints between plasterboard sheets.

Sealant—any tubed silicone or caulk used for sealing along joints such as those between walls and window frames.

Settlement—foundation problems in a house that cause serious cracks and movement in its structure.

Skim—applying top coat of plaster or joint compound to wall surface.

Sole plate—wooden stud creating base or floor fixing for partition wall.

Solvent-based—or oil-based. Term used when referring to the makeup of paint or glaze.

Spacer—divider used between ceramic tiles to keep consistency of distance between each of the tiles.

Split level—where a room has a step in either floor or ceiling levels.

Steel I-beam—Heavy-duty lintels used when a load-bearing wall is removed and two rooms are converted into one.

Stud—wooden uprights used in the construction of a stud wall.

Stud finder—sensor device used for finding position of joists in ceilings or walls. Some may also have different mode that can be used to trace the position of electrical cables or pipes.

Stud wall—wall made of wooden studs and covered in drywall. Used as partition wall in houses. Finished with plaster or drywall compound.

Tap-Con screw—screw designed to fasten into concrete without the need for a wall plug.

Tint—concentrated color supplied in small tubes or containers, used to add color to paint or glaze for paint-effect purposes. Some are universal in that they can be added to both acrylic- and solvent-based paints or glazes.

Toenailing—nailing or screwing at an angle through wood or masonry in order to provide an attachment.

Tongue and groove—interlocking mechanism used to join some types of planking or building board.

Top plate—wood plate creating ceiling attachment or part of stud wall framework.

Vinyl—protective covering on some wallpapers or additive used in paint, to improve their durable and wipe-able properties.

Wall plug—plastic or metal sheath that is inserted into predrilled hole in wall to house screw insertion.

wall plugs

Wall profile—metal plate used to support and tie in block or brick wall when a new wall is being joined to an existing one.

Wall tie—join interior and exterior layer of a cavity wall together.

Tongue-and-groove paneling: this type of wood paneling is useful for covering rough or uneven walls.

index

index

142

acknowledgments

We would like to thank the following individuals for supplying props, advice, and general help throughout the production of this book—Michael and Sue Read, Mike O'Connor, Kevin Hurley, John and Margaret Dearden, and June Parham.

At Murdoch Books (UK) Ltd we would like to extend our gratitude to all those people who have helped to put this book together, but special thanks to Angela Newton, Laura Cullen, Helen Taylor, Iain MacGregor, and Natasha Treloar for their total professionalism and unerring ability to deal with whatever we threw at them.

Tim Ridley and Katrina Moore, once again made all the photographic sessions a pleasure to attend and, as always, a big thank you to them for the long hours, good humour, and patience throughout the project. Finally, many thanks to Adele Parham for feeding the troops at a moment's notice and always being on hand to counsel two manic authors.

The Publisher would like to thank the following: Magnet Windows and Doors, Screwfix, and A&H Brass Limited.

All photography by Tim Ridley and copyright Murdoch Books (UK) Ltd except: p6, p7, and p8 (Elizabeth Whiting Associates), p9 (Murdoch Books®/Meredith), p22 and p23 (Murdoch Books®/Meredith) except p23 bottom right (Elizabeth Whiting Associates), p30 (Corbis), p31 bottom left (Corbis), p32 and p33 (Corbis), p40 and p41 Graham Cole, p55 bottom right (Elizabeth Whiting Associates), p63 bottom right (Elizabeth Whiting Associates), p73 bottom right (Elizabeth Whiting Associates), p93 bottom right (Murdoch Books®/Meredith), p99 bottom right (Murdoch Books®/Meredith), p104 and p105 (Murdoch Books®/Meredith), p119 bottom right (Elizabeth Whiting Associates), p125 (Murdoch Books®/Meredith.

Time-Life Books is a division of Time Life Inc.
TIME-LIFE is a trademark of Time Warner Inc. and affiliated companies.

TIME LIFE INC.
CHAIRMAN AND CHIEF EXECUTIVE OFFICER: Jim Nelson
PRESIDENT AND CHIEF OPERATING OFFICER: Steven Janas
SENIOR EXECUTIVE VICE PRESIDENT AND CHIEF OPERATIONS OFFICER: Mary Davis Holt
SENIOR VICE PRESIDENT AND CHIEF FINANCIAL OFFICER: Christopher Hearing

TIME-LIFE BOOKS
PRESIDENT: Larry Jellen
SENIOR VICE PRESIDENT, NEW MARKETS: Bridget Boel
VICE PRESIDENT, HOME AND HEARTH MARKETS: Nicholas M. DiMarco
VICE PRESIDENT, CONTENT DEVELOPMENT: Jennifer L. Pearce

TIME-LIFE TRADE PUBLISHING
Vice President and Publisher: Neil S. Levin
Senior Sales Director: Richard J. Vreeland
Director, Marketing and Publicity: Inger Forland
Director of Trade Sales: Dana Hobson
Director of Custom Publishing: John Lalor
Director of Rights and Licensing: Olga Vezeris

WALLS & CEILINGS
Director of New Product Development: Carolyn M. Clark
Marketing Director: Nancy L. Gallo
Senior Editor: Linda Bellamy
Director of Design: Kate L. McConnell
Project Editor: Terrell D. Smith
Production Manager: Virginia Reardon
Quality Assurance: Jim King and Stacy L. Eddy

Color separation by Colourscan, Singapore   Printed in Singapore by Tien Wah Press

10 9 8 7 6 5 4 3 2 1

School and library distribution by Time-Life Education, P.O. Box 85026, Richmond, Virginia 23285-5026.
Library of Congress Cataloging-in-Publication Data
Cassell, Julian
   Walls & ceilings / Julian Cassell & Peter Parham.
      p. cm -- (Repair and renovate)
   Includes index.
   ISBN 0-7370-0327-8 (softcover)
      1. Interior walls--Maintenance and repair--Amateurs' manuals. 2. Ceilings--Maintenance and repair--Amateurs' manuals.
   I. Parham, Peter. II Time-Life Books. III. Title. IV. Series.
TH2239 .C37 2001
643'.7--dc21
                          00-046687